Introduction To Machine Learning with TensorFlow.js

Asim Hussain

Table of Contents

Copyright and License

Introduction to Machine Learning with TensorFlow.js

Revision 1.0.0

Dedicated

This book is dedicated to my wonderful wife Zanete Hussain who gives me my strength and for my children who give me hope for a better future.

Thanks

I want to give a special thanks to Robert Dyball, who helped to edit this book and all of my Kickstarter backers; the list of names includes:

- Ahmad McRoumani
- Aishwarya Sharma
- Alexey Sobolev
- Alexis Vassilopoulos
- Antoni Cortés Cejas
- Antonio Rossi
- Anushree Subramani
- Bala Narayanan
- Bart Gerard
- Bharat Patil
- Bhavan Channira
- Bukunmi Odugbesan
- Chris Lidyard
- Chris Simiskey
- Christos Koutsiaris
- Cláudio Teixeira
- Daniel Lucazeau
- Daniel Szprengiel
- David Delaey
- David Gilson
- David Huby
- David Suz Perez
- Dominik Schenk
- Eduardo Mateus Fleck

- Eric Girardet
- Georgii Toroptsev
- Gérôme Grignon
- Giovanni Canzio
- Graeme Falkner
- Hanani Radzi
- Hardanny Wibowo
- Jacek
- Jaeden Chase Hendricks
- Jayce Crowther
- Juan Foegen
- KC Cardakli, PhD
- Kenneth Chang
- Kliment Petrov
- Kuniyoshi Tone
- Larry Bread
- Leonard-Cristian Modoran
- Luca Pugliese
- Mansoor Malik
- Martin Nuc
- Miguel Verissimo
- Muhammad Hammam
- Munzir Suliman
- Naeem Ahmed
- Nataliia Volovod
- Omer Okcuoglu
- paul taylor
- Pritam Bohra

- Raul Filipe Menezes
- Richard Chellew
- Ron Cromberge
- Rowdy Rabouw
- Samuel J Wandler
- Santhosh John
- Sasidhar Vanga
- Simon Patis
- Sri Aurobindo
- Steve Barnett
- Thibaud Dervily
- Timothy Hawk-Walker
- Trevor Cruz
- Tyler Hardy
- Victor Sanchez
- Vikram Balamurugan
- Vlad Kyshkan
- Yogesh Kumar
- Yukito Oda
- Yves Hendseth
- Zain Fathoni

Preface

Early 2018 I was hiking with my friend Elle Haproff[1], and our partners, somewhere in the UK. We had stopped off at a pub to have lunch and rehydrate and starting talking about Machine Learning. We are both JavaScript developers and have a keen interest in Machine Learning. It turned out we had both explored some of the same Javascript Machine Learning libraries available at the time.

We realized that if we were interested, others would be too, so we started a meetup group in London called AI JavaScript London[2].

Fast forward a few months, and Google announced the first version of TensorFlow.js[3], and the JavaScript Machine Learning space went from nascent to mainstream.

I started giving small mini-workshops on TensorFlow.js as part of our meetup group, and over time I had enough mini-workshops to form a full-day workshop, which I started presenting at conferences and other venues.

Over time the workshop evolved, I saw when the room was excited and people engaged, and many other times, I realized when I had moved too fast, and eyes had glazed over.

The result was a lovely balance between learning enough to be useful and engaging enough, so people are excited to complete it.

This book is that workshop, written down.

I hope you enjoy it. It's a fascinating space, be patient with yourselves.

[1] Elle Haproff Twitter https://twitter.com/EleanorHaproff

[2] AI JavaScript London https://www.meetup.com/AI-JavaScript-London/

[3] first version of TensorFlow.js https://medium.com/tensorflow/introducing-tensorflow-js-machine-learning-in-javascript-bf3eab376db

Part I: Introduction

In this section we will talk about the future of JavaScript and Machine Learning and why you might want to learn about the union of these two technologies. I introduce you to the concept of Neural Networks themselves with a simple example as well as TensorFlow and TensorFlow.js. We also cover the setup instructions for all the code samples in this book.

Introduction

With TensorFlow.js, JavaScript and Machine Learning are finally joining forces. Companies like Uber and Airbnb are already using TensorFlow.js in production. I haven't been this energized by new technology in years.

You can already build some fantastic web applications, take a look at these:

- The emoji scavenger hunt[4], a web-based game where you have to take pictures of real-life items matching an emoji.

- The emotion detector app[5], train an ML model to detect the emotion shown in a face.

- You can even train an in-browser self-driving car using the metacar project[6].

Look, Machine Learning is hard. I'm not going to pretend it isn't. However, I plan to make it easy to learn by:

- Teaching you everything you need, **all the maths, from scratch** (no previous knowledge required).

- Teaching you **just the essentials**, focus only on the things that will be useful for you as a JavaScript engineer.

- **Teaching by doing**, we're going to build four different apps from scratch, each getting progressively more complex but each teaching you something important.

Agenda

1. Introduction

   We will cover an overview of Machine Learning and Neural Networks as well as a history of TensorFlow and TensorFlow.js.

2. Project 1: Using a pre-trained model

   In this first project you will learn how to use a pre-trained model and build your first AI-powered application.

3. TensorFlow

Now we will dig deeper into TensorFlow itself we'll cover what Tensors are, how to create them with TensorFlow.js and how to perform basic mathematical calculations using Tensors.

4. Optimization

   In this section we will explain the core function of TensorFlow and what makes up the field of Machine Learning, Optimization. We will learn what a loss function is and how to use TensorFlow.js to optimise some values based on the loss function.

5. Project 2: Linear & Polynomial regression

   In this lecture we will cover what regression is and when would you use it, why we start with regression and how to build your first regression model.

6. Project 3: Recognizing handwritten numbers

   In this section we will start using the layers API from TensorFlow.js and build a much more sophisticated application that recognizes handwritten digits. We will then use the same problem and solve it using a variety of different ML algorithms.

7. Project 4: Transfer Learning

   Finally we bring all that knowledge together into Transfer Learning, we will take a pre-trained model and train a new model on top of it. Transfer Learning is one of the fastest and least computationally intensive ways to make use of Machine Learning in JavaScript.

How to get the best out of this course?

Each application has been selected very carefully; I layer information on carefully and slowly, so you learn TensorFlow.js at a reasonable pace. That's why I recommend you go through this course in order, complete each project before moving onto the next.

Besides, you will only learn if you do, don't imagine you can skim through the material just reading the source code. As I said, Machine Learning is hard; there are no short cuts just well-made training material and a willingness to learn.

[4] emoji scavenger hunt https://emojiscavengerhunt.withgoogle.com/

[5] emotion detector app https://brendansudol.com/faces/

[6] metacar project https://www.metacar-project.com/

Why do JavaScript developers need to learn TensorFlow.js?

People sometimes laugh at me when I tell them I focus on Machine Learning with JavaScript.

The initial reaction is something along the lines of "but... but... JavaScript isn't very fast?".

What's annoying is that they are right, but also completely wrong, and then right again, but for the wrong reasons, let me explain.

Ok, so how does TensorFlow work? You have probably heard a lot about people using Python write with TensorFlow. That's right, well how about this: https://benchmarksgame-team.pages.debian.net/benchmarksgame/fastest/python.html

mandelbrot

source	secs	mem	gz	busy	cpu load
Python 3	170.25	47,568	688	680.12	100% 100% 100% 100%
Node js	4.04	87,468	1122	15.91	99% 98% 98% 98%

Figure 1. Python vs. NodeJS performance

 Yes, JavaScript is much much faster than Python!

What's going on then, why is Python the choice for Machine Learning?

Here is where it gets interesting, whether you are writing some TensorFlow with JavaScript, or Python all your code is doing is creating a **Data Flow Graph**. Once you've created the graph, you don't need JavaScript or Python anymore. A Data Flow Graph executes as fast and optimized C code. You pump some numbers into the graph, lots of computation happens (in code that was written in C and compiled into machine code), and some numbers get popped out. That's it.

So they are completely wrong, whether you are writing in JavaScript or Python, the resulting Data Flow Graph will be the same and will be just as fast when executed. But, annoyingly, they are also entirely right.

When using TensorFlow in the browser, you are using a version that has been re-written from the ground up in JavaScript! So in the browser, calculations are run using JavaScript, and it's a lot slower. However, when running as JavaScript in NodeJS, it's using the C++ version of TensorFlow, so it runs at the same speed as Python.

Why use TensorFlow.js at all?

- So we never expect someone to do intensive number-crunching in the browser.
- We will crunch those numbers and train machine learning models on something much more powerful than a single browser tab.
- Once that model has been trained, we can save it to a JSON file
- And then we can use the model in the browser!
- To use that model in the browser, we need a version of TensorFlow that works all by itself without installing some C++ application. That's why TensorFlow.js was re-written from the ground up as JavaScript, so we could quickly load and run a pre-trained model in the browser.

Summary

Although you could train models using JavaScript and have the same performance as Python (if you used NodeJS), I don't think we'll be doing that with JavaScript.

I believe in the future, we'll work in teams where some of the team will be creating machine learning models using Python. When they are ready, it's up to us, JavaScript developers, to take those models and build an app around it.

That's why I believe we need to learn TensorFlow.js. Machine Learning is the future, and I want to be there before anyone else.

Setup Instructions

Throughout this course, I will be using Visual Studio Code to write and debug JavaScript code.

You don't have to use Visual Studio Code (VS Code), but I recommend that you do just so that you will be able to follow what I am doing.

If you haven't used Visual Studio Code before, it's entirely Free Open Source editor from Microsoft. It comes with many different plugins that you can use to extend its behavior and make your life a little easier.

I will show you how to install and set up Visual Studio Code and then install a recommended plugin called Live Server.

We will be build several demo applications, the starting and completed code for those applications can be found on the code repository associated with this book.

Instructions

Download the sample code

The sample code for this book can be found on GitHub: https://github.com/codecraft-tv/tfjs

You can choose to either download directly from GitHub as a zip using this direct link: https://github.com/codecraft-tv/tfjs/archive/master.zip

Or if you are comfortable with GitHub and the command line `git` you can type:

```
git clone https://github.com/codecraft-tv/tfjs.git
```

This will create into your current folder a folder called `tfjs` and inside there you will find several folders like so:

```
├──── emoji-trainer
├──── image-classification
├──── linear-regression
├──── loss-regression
├──── mnist
├──── parcel-example
├──── polynomial-regression
├──── tensorflow-basics
└──── tensorflow-optimization
```

Each of these folders is a sample project or some sample code you will need in order to complete this book.

Download and Install Visual Studio Code for your Operating System.

Visit https://code.visualstudio.com/ and follow the instructions for how to install VS code on your operating system.

Install the Live Server plugin.

Most of the code examples in this course will run in the browser, so we need a way to launch a local webserver to serve us an index.html file containing our code. There are quite a few ways of doing this, and if you are comfortable with another method, go right ahead and continue using it. I prefer using the Live Server plugin in VS Code.

You can find more info at https://ritwickdey.github.io/vscode-live-server/.

Figure 2. Install Live Server Plugin

1. Open the **Extensions** panel.

2. Search for `Live Server` in the search box.

3. Click the `Live Sever` result.

4. Press the `install` button to add this extension to VS Code.

Using the Live Server plugin.

Now we have it installed we can use the Live Server plugin in several ways, like so.

Mouse

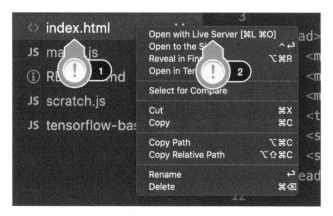

Figure 3. Using the VS Code Live Server Plugin

1. `Right Click` the HTML file you want to serve.

2. Select the menu item "Open with Live Server"

This will launch a web server running in the root of your project on port 5000 and open your default browser, pointing to your HTML page.

Keyboard Shortcuts

You could also start and stop Live Server using the Visual Studio Command Pallette.

Type `Ctrl` + `Shift` + `P` on Windows or `CMD` + `Shift` + `P` on Mac.

This will bring up the command pallette, start typing "Live Server" and you will see the option "Live Server: Open With Live Server" appear, select that option.

What is a Neural Network?

A Neural Network has a basis in biology. This is a neuron, our brains have a least one of these:

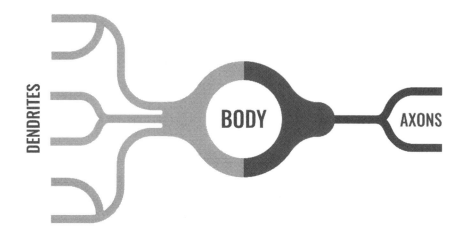

Figure 4. Biological Neuron

In the center is the Body, it has some Dendrites flowing in and some Axons flowing out. If **enough** electricity flows in via the Dendrites, the Body gets triggered and pushes some electricity out through the Axons. If we stick enough of these together (about 100 billion[7]), we get a Brain.

That's pretty much it.

If you code this up in JavaScript, you might conceptually build something like this.

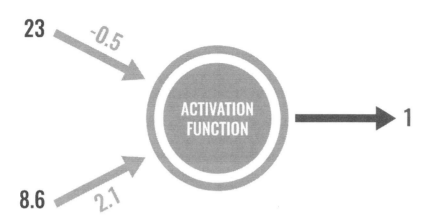

Figure 5. Artificial Neuron

We create an Acyclic Graph[8], big words, but that means a node acts as our Body with some edges (Dendrites and Axons) going in and out and the edges can't go back around and point back at itself.

We pump a *number* into each edge; this is the amount of *electricity* we are sending through it, it's perhaps the *strength signal* from a sensor in our Body.

But some electricity is more important that other electricity. For example, if this neuron was my *should I open my umbrella neuron* the signal for *I'm feeling rain on my head* is more important than the signal *I see clouds*. To model this in our artificial neuron, we use weights; this is a number that we assign to each edge.

To model how the Body decides if enough electricity has been pumped in and how much to pump back out, we use something called an activation function.

To understand what happens next, take a look at this equation:

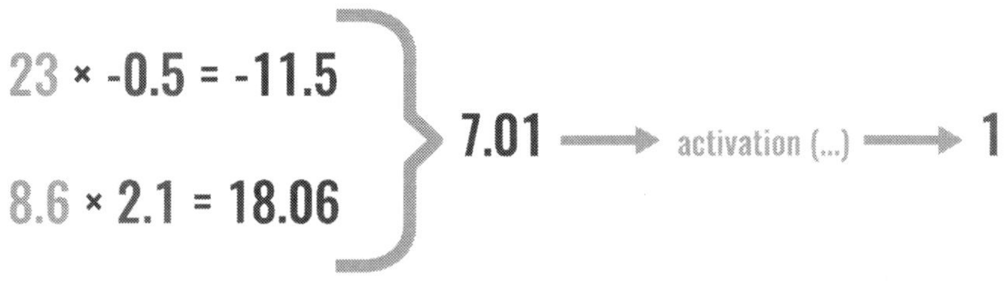

$$23 \times -0.5 = -11.5$$

$$8.6 \times 2.1 = 18.06$$

$$\left.\begin{matrix} \end{matrix}\right\} \quad 7.01 \longrightarrow \text{activation} (...) \longrightarrow 1$$

Figure 6. Simple neuron equation

1. We multiply the `electricity` by the `weight` and add them all up for the inputs (the Dendrites).

2. To model the Body we pass that number into our `activation function` and whatever number that returns is what we pass out through the output edges, the *Axons*.

There are lots of different types of activation functions, and this is a simple binary one:

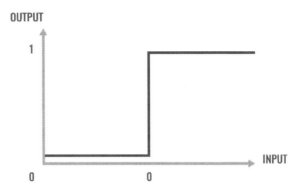

Figure 7. Binary activation function

If the input signal is above 0, we pass out 1. If the input signal is less than 0, we pass out -1. It's simple, it's easy to calculate, but it results in sharp changes to the output for minimal changes to the input.

There are others, another popular one is the **hyperbolic tanh**, resulting in a much smoother change in the output signal for a change in the input signal.

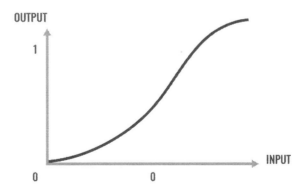

Figure 8. Tanh activation function

Another popular one is *RELU*, Rectified Linear Unit. This has some non-linearity but is much easier to calculate than TanH by a computer so is often used as a compromise.

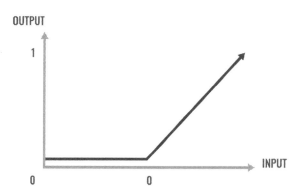

Figure 9. RELU activation function

Layered Neural Network

If you connect enough of these artificial neurons, you get a neural network.

This is what we call a simple four-layer feed-forward densely connected neural network:

That's a lot of words, let's break it down step by step.

4 Layer

There are four layers of neurons in this network. The *Purple* input layer on the left, the *Red* output layer on the right, and two what we call *Hidden* layers in between.

Feed Forward

Feed forward[9] means that at no point do the connections form a cycle; each layer connects only to the next layer.

There is nothing *tricky* where an output edge snakes back behind and becomes an input in an earlier node. There are Neural Networks that are architected like this, for instance, a Recurrent Neural Network[10], but we won't be covering that in this course.

Densely Connected

Densely Connected means that each node in one layer connects to each node in the next layer. For example, this is densely connected:

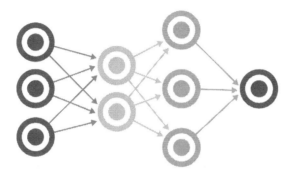

Figure 10. Densely connected neural network

This is sparsely connected:

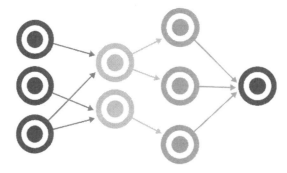

Figure 11. Sparsely connected neural network

Using a Neural Network

Imagine this neural network is now a more sophisticated version of my *how wet am I about to get?* predictor.

The input layer takes in, as signals, some information.

1. The number of raindrops detected per second on a sensor.
2. How cloudy it is on a scale of 0 to 10, 10 being thunderstorm and 0 being a warm sunny day.
3. The current temperature.

The output node pumps out the predicted cm of rain that will fall in the next hour.

For all the activation functions, we used TanH.

If you have a **fully trained** Neural Network, then it's simple.

We pump in the current values of our signals into the input layer, it gets multiplied by the weights, passed through activation functions all the way through until it outputs a number.

A Neural Network is just a mathematical function.

I mentally think of it like so:

```
function rainPredictor(
    rainDropsPerSecond,
    cloudyness,
    temperature)
{
    let cmsOfRainInNextHour = 0;

    // maths stuff involving all those weights

    return cmsOfRainInNextHour;
}
```

The critical thing is that the *stuff* in the code comment above is a single mathematical expression rather than a complex workflow with conditionals, you won't find if's and else's in a Neural Network.

That's it, that's all you need to do to use a Neural Network.

Training a Neural Network

The real question is *what should we use as the weights?*. The weights are crucial to everything, the weights *are* the Neural Network.

When we first create our network, we initialize the weights with random numbers, usually between 0 and 1.

So an untrained neural network is going to do a pretty lousy job of predicting rain.

Training a Neural Network is the process of tuning those weights so that the neural network gets better at pumping out useful numbers on the other side.

There are several ways of training a neural network, but the most popular and most accessible is to use supervised learning. This is like learning by trial and error. To do this, we need what's called a labeled data set.

We need some historical data where for a given set of inputs we know what the output was, like so:

Drops/s	Cloudy	Temp	Rain CM
0	1.2	23	0
1.2	4.5	15	1.2

The first line is one example, we have 0 drops per second, it's not very cloudy, and it's pretty sunny, and we can see an hour later that 0 cm of rain fell.

The second line shows a more rainy example.

The first three columns are what we call *features*; these are the inputs to our neural network model, to our function. The last column is our *label*; this is what we would want our correctly trained neural network to output if we pumped in the input *features*.

For each line of our example data, we feed those numbers into our untrained model; we let it multiply all the way through and see what it outputs on the other side.

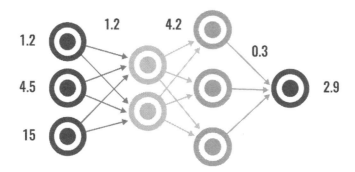

Figure 12. Using a neural network

That's our untrained model's prediction; we compare that to the real CM of rainfall from the last column in the dataset.

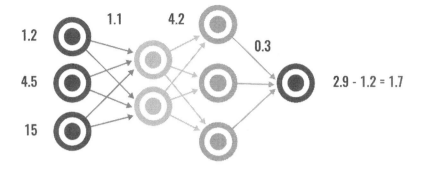

Figure 13. How accurate is our neural network

We calculate how wrong our Neural Network is, we need that number we call that the *loss*.

We pump in all our examples and get a total *loss*.

We then use a technique called **Back Propagation**; this adjusts the weights depending on how wrong our Neural Network was and tweaks the weights slightly in the right direction.

That's one *epoch*, one iteration, of training through all the data. We go through all our data again and again and do the back propagation again and again. Each time it tweaks the weights in the right direction to make our neural network more accurate.

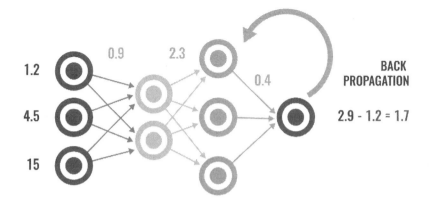

Figure 14. Training our neural network

Eventually, we end up with a trained neural network that's pretty accurate, so when I'm out and about, I can use it to predict the rain and whether I should open my umbrella.

Summary

That was a pretty simple Neural Network. They can get much more complicated than that, but the concepts and ideas remain the same.

- A neural network is a mathematical function, an expression, the challenge is how to represent your problem as a mathematical function.

- It contains some weights, which we initialize with random numbers; that's why an untrained model doesn't do a very good job.

- Training a neural network is the process of tuning those weights, so it gets better at predicting the right results.

- We initially some nodes with edges and weights.

- The technique we will be using (the simplest and the most popular) is supervised learning, where we take sample data with known results and train the neural network using that.

[7] about 100 billion https://www.theguardian.com/science/blog/2012/feb/28/how-many-neurons-human-

brain

[8] Acyclic Graph http://mathworld.wolfram.com/AcyclicGraph.html

[9] Feed forward https://en.wikipedia.org/wiki/Feedforward_neural_network

[10] Recurrent Neural Network https://en.wikipedia.org/wiki/Recurrent_neural_network

What is TensorFlow?

TensorFlow (https://www.tensorflow.org/) itself is an incredibly powerful machine learning and deep learning library. It allows you to build these constructs called Data Flow Graphs, which represent a Machine Learning model. It was developed by Google Brain for internal use, and open-sourced in November 2015.

It allows you to define mathematical functions and scale the execution of those functions in parallel across multiple cores on your CPU, multiple cores on a GPU, as well as across multiple computers.

Your GPU, Graphics Processing Unit, is a card inside your computer designed to figure out how to draw things on a screen. It's like a CPU but a lot less general-purpose, it can do one thing but do that thing well and now really fast. It does that by running 100s of calculations in parallel; it just happens that these types of calculations are also perfect for machine learning.

You may hear the term GPU being used a lot with Machine Learning; your graphics card is more useful to you in machine learning than your main CPU.

What is TensorFlow.js?

Here is where it gets exciting, TensorFlow is built using C++, it's incredibly fast, but that doesn't help you so much if you are a JavaScript developer.

In 2018 Google announced TensorFlow.js (https://www.tensorflow.org/js/). I have to admit that at first, I assumed that TensorFlow.js was just a Node.js binding to TensorFlow. I *thought* you could only use TensorFlow.js if TensorFlow was installed on your computer and you could only use it from Node.js, not from the browser. I was wrong on both counts.

TensorFlow.js is TensorFlow re-written from the ground up in JavaScript.

That deserves repeating, *"TensorFlow.js is TensorFlow re-written from the ground up in JavaScript"*.

What this means is that to use TensorFlow.js you **don't need to install any dependencies**.

You only need to import one package, like so:

```
import * as ts from '@tensroflow/tfjs';
```

Or, even simpler, you can just add one script tag in your HTML file, like so:

```
<script src=
"https://cdn.jsdelivr.net/npm/@tensorflow/tfjs/dist/tf.min.js"></script>
```

That's it, that's all you need to get started doing Machine Learning in the browser.

Core API vs. Layers API

The original TensorFlow Python API can be used for a wide variety of purposes, anything requiring large amounts of parallel mathematical calculations but is pretty low level.

The community responded by building higher-level packages like keras[11], which take care of a lot of the boilerplate in TensorFlow writing Neural Networks.

The TensorFlow.js library consists of two different packages, the first is a flexible low-level **core** API, which is syntactically very similar to the TensorFlow Python API.

The core API is low level, so if **all** you are building is a Neural Network, then you can end up writing lots of boilerplate code for each project.

For TensorFlow.js the team decided to incorporate a *Keras* style API as part of the package, and it's called the **layers** API.

 In this course, we will be covering the core API so we can build a good understanding of the internals, and then we will move onto using the layers API.

Node.js TensorFlow vs Browser TensorFlow.js

The version of TensorFlow.js I discuss above I will refer to as *browser* TensorFlow.js; however, that is inaccurate, it can be used in the browser OR within Node.js.

There is a crucial difference between the browser version of TensorFlow.js and the version you can use with Node.js.

When used in the browser, it will use the GPU to perform calculations through the browsers Web GL API. This can result in a 100x performance improvement vs. running on the vanilla CPU of your computer.

When used via Node.js, it will only use the vanilla CPU,

To perform slightly faster via Node.js you can use this package:

```
import * as tf from '@tensorflow/tfjs-node'
```

This installs the TensorFlow binary into your node_modules folder. You are controlling a standard TensorFlow instance via JavaScript bindings.

If you are running on Linux, you can use the GPU accelerated version of TensorFlow.js via:

```
import * as tf from '@tensorflow/tfjs-node-gpu'
```

This will run calculations on the GPU with CUDA[12], resulting again in significant speed improvement.

You can find more information about how to run TensorFlow.js from within Node.js from this link https://www.tensorflow.org/js/guide/nodejs.

[11] keras https://keras.io

[12] CUDA https://blogs.nvidia.com/blog/2012/09/10/what-is-cuda-2/

Part II: Run Existing Machine Learning Models

We will build our first application using a **pre-trained** MobileNet model. We then drill into the MobileNet model in-depth and discuss how it might take inputs and the actual format of it's outputs.

Pre-Trained Models

As mentioned before, you can use TensorFlow.js to train models *from scratch* or load a model trained previously and use it. We call this using a model in inference mode[13], and that's what we're going to cover in this section.

Where can you find pre-trained models?

The easiest place to get started is to use one of the pre-trained models found on the TensorFlow.js website

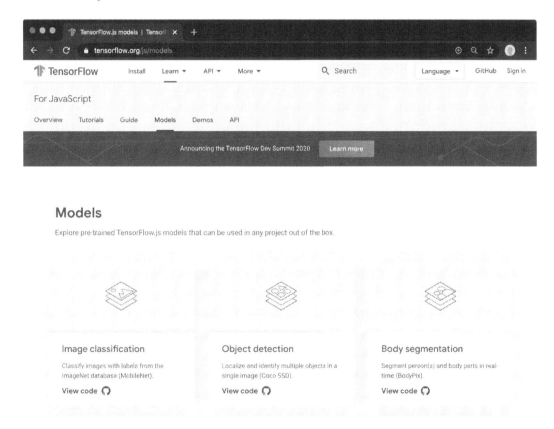

You can find links to a set of different pre-trained models that have been curated and ensure work properly with TensorFlow.js.

How to load one of these models

Each model is a little different, so it's worth reading it's documentation. Taking a look at the Image Classification[14] example, to begin with, we usually have two methods.

Using script tags

The first is to use a script tag.

For example to use the MobileNet Image Classification Model[15] we need to add two script tags to our HTML, like so:

```
<script src="https://cdn.jsdelivr.net/npm/@tensorflow/tfjs@1.0.1">
</script>

<script src="https://cdn.jsdelivr.net/npm/@tensorflow-
models/mobilenet@1.0.0"> </script>
```

The first script tag loads TensorFlow.js itself, the second script tag loads mobilenet library, which is based on TensorFlow.js; that's why you need to load TensorFLow.js first.

Using script tags is the easiest; it's how we'll be using pre-trained models in all our demos in this course. In a more complex production application, I recommend using a JavaScript bundler of some form.

Using a bundler

As your application gets more substantial, you may want to bundle up all the JavaScript files in your project into one and have one script tag in your project. I won't be going into great depth here; there are several different bundlers of various complexity and feature sizes; I will demonstrate how to use one called Parcel.

To use a bundler you need to be comfortable with Node.js, how to install packages and run commands from the command line.

If you were using the bundler Parcel.js[16] for instance, you would do something like this:

In your HTML file include your main javascript file, like so:

```
<html>
    <body>
        <script src="./main.js"></script>
    </body>
</html>
```

Then in your main.js file, you can use ES6 `import` statements to include the libraries that you need, for mobilenet this would be something along the lines of:

```
import "regenerator-runtime/runtime";

import * as mobilenet from '@tensorflow-models/mobilenet';

(async function () {
    // Load the model.
    const model = await mobilenet.load();

    // Once it's loaded you can call mobilenet functions
})();
```

 import "regenerator-runtime/runtime"; is needed to resolve an issue[17] with how Parcel handles async/await with imports.

First install parcel like so:

```
npm install -g parcel-bundler
```

Then in the project folder create a blank package file with:

```
npm init -y
```

and then finally run:

```
parcel index.html
```

This will discover all the dependant packages, create a folder called `dist` with index.html and a single javascript file will all the dependant packages rolled up into one.

You can find more information about using Parcel from their getting started[18] page.

[13] inference mode https://blogs.nvidia.com/blog/2016/08/22/difference-deep-learning-training-inference-ai/

[14] Image Classification https://github.com/tensorflow/tfjs-models/tree/master/mobilenet

[15] MobileNet Image Classification Model https://github.com/tensorflow/tfjs-models/tree/master/mobilenet

[16] Parcel.js https://parceljs.org/

[17] resolve an issue https://medium.com/@binyamin/enabling-async-await-and-generator-functions-in-babel-node-and-express-71e941b183e2

[18] getting started https://parceljs.org/getting_started.html

Image Classification

The task of trying to figure out **what** is in an image is called **image classification**, we are trying to find to which **class** this image belongs.

There are several different image classification models out there, one of the most popular is MobileNet, the clue is in the name. Models can become quite large, MobileNet is optimized to be small, it's about 20mb in total which in the land of image classification models is pretty tiny.

In this example we'll build a small app that uses MobileNet to figure out what's your webcam is pointing at, it will look something like so:

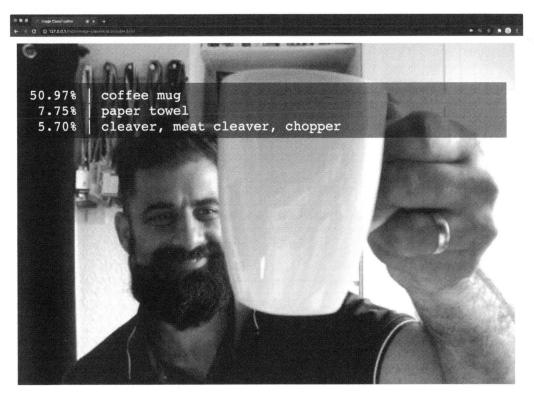

Figure 15. Our application recognizes a coffee mug

In this lecture, I'll take you through building an app like that step by step.

MobileNet

We will be using a version of MobileNet that has already been optimized and converted for use in TensorFlow.js.

https://github.com/tensorflow/tfjs-models/tree/master/mobilenet

You can use this model both the ways I have shown in previous lectures, either loading it via `script` tags or installing it via `npm` and using a bundler. We'll be loading it via `script` tags for simplicity.

Code

The code for this project is in the `image-classification` folder in the source code repository for this book.

Inside that folder, you will find four files like so:

```
.
├── index.html      ❶
├── utils.js        ❷
├── style.css       ❸
├── start.js        ❹
└── completed.js    ❺
```

❶ `index.html` contains the HTML for our project and loads the other JavaScript and CSS files.

❷ `utils.js` is just some utility classes for rendering the results to the screen, feel free to browse, but we won't be covering the contents of those in this book.

❸ `style.css` contains some styles for use with the application, we won't be going into the details of styling in this course.

❹ `start.js` is the JavaScript file we are going to start with. There is some boilerplate code there to get you started, but none of the TensorFlow.js code is present, we'll be adding that in as we go along.

❺ `completed.js` is the completed JavaScript code, if you get stuck, I recommend checking our this file to see where you might have gone wrong.

The start.js file has several TODO comment blocks, as we continue with this lecture I will leave it to you to fill out those TODO blocks and build out the application. The amount of code you will have to write is trivial.

Loading the JavaScript

In our example we are loading TensorFlow.js and MobileNet using <script> tags in the <head> of index.html, like so:

```html
<!-- Load TensorFlow.js. This is required to use MobileNet. -->
<script src="https://cdn.jsdelivr.net/npm/@tensorflow/tfjs"></script>

<!-- Load the MobileNet model. -->
<script src="https://cdn.jsdelivr.net/npm/@tensorflow-models/mobilenet"></script>

<script src="utils.js"></script>
<script src="start.js"></script>
```

If you want to use a bundler, feel free to do so. Refer to **Using a bundler** in the **Pre-Trained Models** lecture for more information.

We need to load TensorFlow.js first, **before** we load the MobileNet files. This is one of the disadvantages of using script tags; you need to know the order that javascript files need to be included, a bundler handles this for you.

Understanding the HTML

The body of our html looks like so:

```
<div class="container">
  <video id="video"> ❶
    Video stream not available.
  </video>
  <div class="overlay"> ❷
    <pre id="predictions"></pre>
  </div>
</div>
```

❶ <video> is the HTML element that will load and display the webcam's contents.

❷ This div contains the predictions of what the webcam is seeing.

Loading mobilenet

In our sample code we will be initializing the load of MobileNet in our main function. The MobileNet JavaScript file we loaded via our <script> tags is not the whole of MobileNet, it's just the controlling code. MobileNet itself, the actual trained model, is a set of data files many megabytes large, which needed to be loaded over the internet before you can use MobileNet. We initialize this loading like so:

```
let model = null; ❶
async function main() {
    // Initialize MobileNet and wait for is to load all it's required data
files over the internet
    model = await mobilenet.load(); ❷
    await startCamera(); ❸
}
main();
```

❶ We keep a reference to our model so we can use it in other functions.

❷ This line starts loading the MobileNets data files over the network and waits for then to be loaded before moving to the next line.

❸ This starts the camera and runs the rest of our code.

In total, MobileNet is 18mb of data, which might seem like a lot, but for a neural network that can classify what's in an image, it's pretty small. If we were to look in the browser's network panel right now, we would see several shard files loaded.

This is the MobileNet data chunked into 4mb files loading over the network, like so:

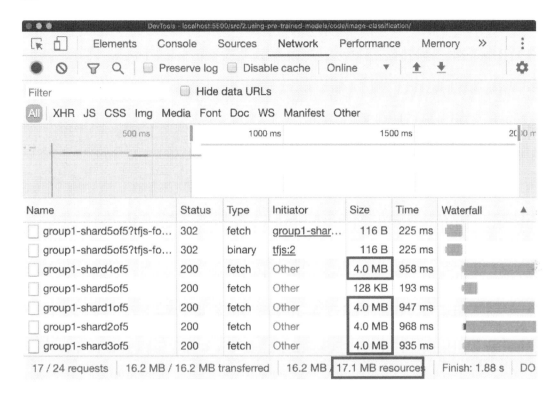

Start Camera

The startCamera() function does the bulk of the work, let's break down the code line by line:

```
async function startCamera() {
    let videoElement = document.getElementById("video"); ❶
    const camera = await tf.data.webcam(videoElement); ❷

    setInterval(async () => { ❸
        const image = await camera.capture(); ❹
        let predictions = await model.classify(image); ❺

        renderPredictions(predictions); ❻

        const logits = await model.infer(image); ❼
        logits.print();
    }, 1000);
}
```

❶ Gets the <video> HTML element from the document.

❷ This helper function from the TensorFlow.js library initializes the camera and starts it running i.e., this line makes the video element start showing the contents of your webcam.

❸ Every second we want to grab a still from the video and use MobileNet to figure out what's inside it, so we use the setInterval(⋯, 1000) function with a 1000 ms timer.

❹ We capture a still image from the video stream.

❺ MobileNet comes with a helper classify function, which, if passed an image will return information about what it thinks is in the image.

❻ renderPredictions is a helper function in util.js which pretty prints the output from MobileNet on screen.

❼ The infer function returns the raw output from the MobileNet model.

The above code is all you need to create an app that can detect what's in an image, like so:

```
11.86% | spatula
10.19% | syringe
 6.16% | lampshade, lamp shade
```

However, after using the app for a while, you might notice that the guesses are quite often wrong. In the next lecture, we'll look into why that might be the case, the raw output of a model, and how to build a Neural Network model that classifies things.

MobileNet Inputs and Outputs

The MobileNet app you built, although incredibly cool, wasn't that good at predicting what's inside an image. In this lecture, we'll take a look at why and by the end, you'll understand how a classification model is structured, the inputs and the outputs.

Classes

The MobileNet model is a type of *classification* model given a set of inputs (the image); it can decide what **class** they belong to, for example, *toilet tissue*.

Taking a look at the MobileNet code, there is a file called `imagenet_classes.ts` which you can find online here: https://github.com/tensorflow/tfjs-models/blob/master/mobilenet/src/imagenet_classes.ts

Inside that file you will find an object that lists 1000 *things*, like so:

```
export const IMAGENET_CLASSES: {[classId: number]: string} = {
  0: 'tench, Tinca tinca',
  1: 'goldfish, Carassius auratus',
  2: 'great white shark, white shark, man-eater, man-eating shark,
Carcharodon carcharias',
    .

    .

    .
  996: 'hen-of-the-woods, hen of the woods, Polyporus frondosus, Grifola '
+
      'frondosa',
  997: 'bolete',
  998: 'ear, spike, capitulum',
  999: 'toilet tissue, toilet paper, bathroom tissue'
};
```

The MobileNet model has been trained to detect only 1000 *things* in the world. Models that can identify a lot more in an image exist; however, they are very large. MobileNet, as the name suggests, has been optimized so that the model size is small, it's currently about 18 MB of data which for use in a mobile context, or even at a stretch in a web context, is fine.

You can also see that each textual description has a number associated with it, so 999 equals 'toilet tissue, toilet paper, bathroom tissue'.

Inputs and Outputs

What does the model take as inputs, and what does it output?

We saw from the previous lecture that the model took as inputs an image, like so:

```
const image = await camera.capture();
let predictions = await model.classify(image)
```

model.classify is just a helper function, the actual code used to pump data into a model and grab its outputs is called model.infer and we can use it like so:

```
const logits = await model.infer(image);
logits.print();
```

Calling infer returns for us something which we call logits. You can console.log(logits) but it won't reveal any useful data; it's a type of something called a Tensor. To get a Tensor to print something useful to the console we need to use the print() function, it will print something like so:

```
Tensor
     [[0.7322746, 0.0774543, 0.609502, ..., -4.9255857, 2.2073834,
6.5471358],]
```

Logits are the raw numerical output of the model; you can see it's printing out three numbers then ⋯ then three other numbers. Tensors can be huge and printing them out problematic, so the print function just prints the first and last three numbers.

To see the size and shape of the Tensor we can log the shape property, like so:

```
const logits = await model.infer(image);
console.log(logits.shape);
logits.print();
```

This will print out [1, 1000] to the console, which means 1 column and 1000 rows.

So our logits Tensor contains 1000 numbers, this might give a clue to what the output of our model might be?

Classification Outputs

To simplify, let's imagine we have a model that's trained only to detect if a black and white image is of a *cat* or a *dog*.

Perhaps we break the image down into a set of black and white pixels with values ranging from 0 for black and 255 for white and then pass those is as inputs into our model.

What would the output be if we passed an image of a cat to the model? At first, you might guess that the model might return the string "cat", like so:

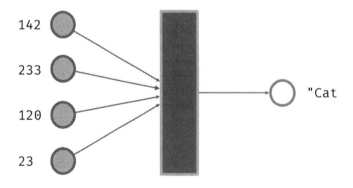

Figure 16. Does a model output the string "cat"?

However, that's not how classification models work; models are just equations we pump some numbers in, it does various forms of maths and pumps some numbers out, so the output has to be *numbers*.

You then might assume that the model outputs a number, perhaps 1 for Cat and 2 for Dog, like so:

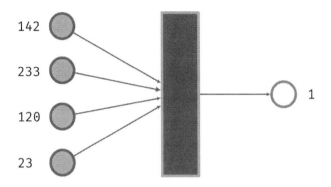

Figure 17. Does a model output the number 1?

This isn't quite how a classification model works, instead for *each* class it outputs a number, like so:

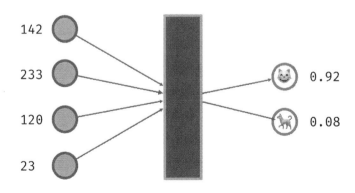

Figure 18. The model outputs a probability distribution?

Each number is related to the *probability* of that class being the one that matches the inputs.

Softmax

Looking back at the output of our MobileNet model, we can see that we are outputting 1000 numbers. Each of these numbers maps to one element in our IMAGENET_CLASSES object.

```
Tensor
    [[0.7322746, 0.0774543, 0.609502, ..., -4.9255857, 2.2073834,
6.5471358],]
```

But they don't look like probabilities; some of them are even negative.

With classification models, we take the raw outputs and pass them through a softmax function. Softmax[19] is a mathematical function that turns an array of numbers into a probability distribution ranging from 0 to 1; you can find out more details about how softmax works mathematically in the article Understand the Softmax Function in Minutes[20].

TensorFlow.js comes with a handy softmax() function which we can use like so:

```
const logits = await model.infer(image);
logits.softmax().print();
```

And this prints out something like:

```
Tensor
    [[0.0000087, 0.0000045, 0.0000077, ..., 0, 0.0000378, 0.0029015],]
```

Which looks far more like a probability distribution, all the numbers add up to one, and the number with the highest probability is what it thinks the image is.

Summary

Models take as inputs numbers and output numbers. Everything you want to solve in Machine Learning needs to be represented in the domain of numbers. This is one of the core challenges of Machine Learning, how to take a problem domain and represent it in numerical form? For a classification model the typical solution is to use a softmax function which gives a probability for what *class* you think the *inputs* fall into.

[19] Softmax https://en.wikipedia.org/wiki/Softmax_function

[20] Understand the Softmax Function in Minutes https://medium.com/data-science-bootcamp/understand-the-softmax-function-in-minutes-f3a59641e86d

Part III: Tensors

Before we can begin to build and train our models, we need to dig into the raw building blocks of TensorFlow, Tensors. We cover how to create them, the operations you can perform on them, and a standard method of calculating the error between two arrays, Mean Squared Error. We then cover TensorFlow.js itself and demonstrate how to use TensorFlow.js to learn the optimum values for variables in a function.

What are Tensors?

Tensors are the building blocks of a machine learning model. They are nothing to be scared of; you've most likely been using them for a while but have never called them *Tensors*.

They are a set of numbers of a specific size and shape.

So far, we've explained how neural network models are just functions that manipulate numbers, a set of input numbers of a specific size, into a set of output numbers into another size and shape. Tensors are how we represent those numbers, the inputs, the outputs, and everything in between.

Rank

The dimensionality of a Tensor we call it's *rank*.

A 1D Tensor (or rank 1 Tensor) is just an array, like so:

1D TENSOR / VECTOR

A 2D Tensor (or rank 2 Tensor) is just a 2-dimensional array, so an array of arrays, like so:

2D TENSOR / MATRIX

8	29	14	4
-10	0	-4	-2
6	24	21	-6
-8	11	-10	-10

A 3D Tensor (or rank 3 Tensor) is a cube. An array of arrays of arrays, like so:

3D TENSOR / CUBE

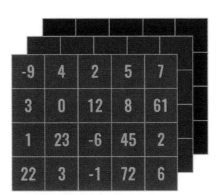

Everything after 3D becomes harder to conceptualize, but let's try. A 4D Tensor is an array of 3D Tensors, like so:

4D TENSOR / VECTOR OF CUBES

A 5D Tensor is an array of 4D Tensors, like so:

5D TENSOR / MATRIX OF CUBES

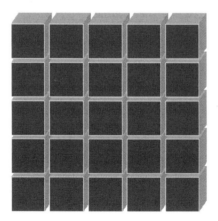

Shape

The size of each dimension in a Tensor we call its shape. For example, a Tensor to represent a black and white image would have the shape [width, height, colors].

For a 640 x 480 pixel black and white image, the shape would be [640,480, 1].

colors in this case would be of size 1; in a black and white image, the only color is black; in a color image, the size might be 3 with a value for red, green, and blue.

The rank of the Tensor is 3; it's a 3D Tensor.

How to represent a data set of images?

For one type of machine learning, supervised learning[21], we provide large sets of training data for our machine learning models.

We represent a single black and white image as a 3D Tensor of shape [width, height, color].

We represent a set of 1000 black and white image as a 4D Tensor of shape [sample_size, width, height, color].

For example, a set of 1000, 640 x 480 pixel black and white images would be represented as 4D Tensor of Shape [1000, 640, 480, 1].

Summary

Tensors are just buckets of numbers of a specific shape and a certain rank (dimensionality). Tensors are used in Machine Learning with TensorFlow to represent input data and output data (and everything in between) in Machine Learning models.

[21] supervised learning https://en.wikipedia.org/wiki/Supervised_learning

Creating Tensors

We've covered the basic concept of Tensors in the previous lecture. In this lecture, we are going to learn how you use them in practice with TensorFlow.js. There will be a short quiz at the end.

Code

The code for this lecture, and the next lecture on operations, is in the tensorflow-basics folder in the source code associated with this course.

That folder has three files, like so:

```
.
├─── index.html    ❶
├─── main.js       ❷
└─── scratch.js    ❸
```

❶ This index.html file loads tensorflow.js and also just the scratch.js file.

❷ This file contains all the completed code for this lecture.

❸ This file should be empty.

Open the index.html as we taught in the setup-instructions lecture and then open the console in the browser, this is where the messages will go.

Add your code to scratch.js and refresh the browser to execute it. If you have problems, check main.js to see the correct completed code.

Creating a Tensor

We create a Tensor using the tf.tensor function like so:

```
var a = tf.tensor([1, 2, 3]);    ❶
console.log(a.rank);             ❷
console.log(a.shape);            ❸
```

❶ Creates a 1D tensor of size 3.

❷ rank returns the rank (dimensionality) of a Tensor, for our example will return 1.

❸ shape returns the size of each of the dimensions; for our example, this returns just [3].

Getting data from the Tensor

Now we want to look at the Tensor, print it out, and access the data we passed in.

You might try printing out the Tensor like so:

```
console.log(a);
```

But this would print out something like so:

```
t {kept: false, isDisposedInternal: false, shape: Array(1), dtype:
"float32", size: 3, ···}
```

It's the Tensor object, but not the data the Tensor holds.

To print out the data inside a Tensor, we have a helper function called print() which we use like so:

```
a.print();
```

This will print to the console something like:

```
Tensor
    [1, 2, 3]
```

But that's just for logging if you want to get access to the data itself you need to use another function called dataSync(), like so:

```
let data = a.dataSync();
console.log(data);
```

Which will print out something like so:

```
Float32Array(3) [1, 2, 3]
```

`data` in this case is a standard JavaScript floating-point array that you can use as you would use any other array.

Explicitly defining the rank

In the above example, `tf.tensor` *guesses* the rank of the Tensor based on the shape of the input data passed in, but you can be more explicit and specify the exact rank you are expecting in the input data like so:

```
var a = tf.tensor1d([1, 2, 3]);
console.log(a.rank);
console.log(a.shape);
a.print();
```

 In this example we are using `tf.tensor1d` instead of `tf.tensor`.

If we use a specific rank tensor like `tf.tensor1d` we can catch simple errors like the one below:

```
var a = tf.tensor1d([[1, 2, 3]]);
```

The above will print an error to the console, the reason might be hard to see, but if you look closely you will see that instead of passing a 1D array we are passing in a 2D array like so:

`[[1, 2, 3]]`

or to make it even easier to see:

```
[
    [1, 2, 3]
]
```

Another error that you may commonly encounter is when the input data's shape is not complete, like so:

```
var a = tf.tensor([[1, 2], [3]]);
```

To fix the above, we need to make the shape the same size for all the `axis`, like so:

```
var a = tf.tensor([[1, 2], [3, 4]]);
```

Explicitly providing the shape

Finally you can be even more explicit and provide the shape yourself, like so:

```
var a = tf.tensor(
    [1, 2, 3, 4],    ❶
    [2, 2]           ❷
);
```

❶ We give it the raw data as a 1D array.

❷ We additionally give the shape of the data, this is a rank 2, a 2D Tensor.

This is the typical pattern when dealing with non-trivial shapes of data. It's tough for the human eye and mind to understand and recognize shapes beyond 2D. So we would provide the data as a 1D array and explicitly think about and talk about the shape.

 Get used to talking about Tensors and reasoning about them in terms of their *shape* and *rank*.

Quiz

Question

In the **What are Tensors?** lecture, we gave an example of a set of 100, 640 x 480 pixel black and white images.

Imagine all the data was provided as a 1D array called data, like so:

```
var data = Array(100*640*480).fill(1); ❶
```

❶ This creates an array of size 100*640*480 where each value is the number 1

How would you represent that data set as a Tensor?

Solution

If you remember from the **What are Tensors?** lecture we defined the shape as [sample_size, width, height, colors]. For our specific example, the shape would then be [100, 640, 480, 1], colors is 1 because our image only has one color *black*.

We can then create a Tensor that represents this image like so:

```
var a = tf.tensor(data, [100, 640, 480, 1]);
```

We could be even more explicit by using tf.tensor4D and specifying the rank like so:

```
var a = tf.tensor4d(data, [100, 640, 480, 1]);
```

If you specified the wrong shape, for instance, if you used the shape [100, 640, 480, 2] then you would get an error in the console like so:

```
`Uncaught Error: Based on the provided shape, [100,640,480,2], the tensor
should have 61440000 values but has 30720000`
```

Summary

You can create Tensors using the tf.tensor function. It guesses the shape and rank of the Tensor from the input data, or you can be more explicit by providing the shape as the second parameter by using one of the rank specific tensor creation functions like tf.tensor4d.

The standard model for non-trivial use cases is to provide the data as a 1D array and then specify the shape yourself rather than trying to morph the data into the shape you expect and having TensorFlow try to guess the shape of the Tensor from the shape of your data.

Tensor Operations

You can perform operations on Tensors, such as addition, which return new Tensors. TensorFlow.js has an extensive library[22] of available operations, which you are encouraged to review. In this course, we will only be covering the *essential* operations required to understand the example applications we are building.

Addition

We perform element-wise addition via the add function; this sums two Tensors together using *pair wise* addition, like so:

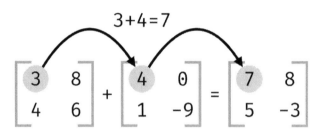

Figure 19. Image of pairwise addition

```
var a = tf.tensor([3, 8, 4, 6], [2, 2]);
var b = tf.tensor([4, 0, 1, -9], [2, 2]);
a.add(b).print();
```

The shape of both the Tensors should be the same to perform element wise addition otherwise it will print an error to the console, like so:

```
var a = tf.tensor([3, 8, 4, 6], [2, 2]);
var b = tf.tensor([4, 0, 1], [2, 1]);
a.add(b).print(); // This will print an error
```

Broadcasting

When the shapes allow, TensorFlow.js will perform an action called *broadcasting* instead of reporting an error, like so:

```
var a = tf.tensor([3, 8, 4, 6], [2, 2]);
var b = tf.tensor([4, 0], [2]);
a.add(b).print();
```

Even though the shape of a and b are different, the add operation completed successfully and resulted in a Tensor like so:

```
Tensor
    [[7, 8],
     [8, 6]]
```

Broadcasting is the process of *automatically adjusting* matrices to have compatible shapes for arithmetic operations.

Broadcasting means that an operation like so:

```
var a = tf.tensor([3, 8, 4, 6], [2, 2]);
var b = tf.tensor([4, 0], [2]);
a.add(b).print();
```

Was transformed internally into:

```
var a = tf.tensor([3, 8, 4, 6], [2, 2]);
var b = tf.tensor([4, 0, 4, 0], [2, 2]);
a.add(b).print();
```

The data was copied in b, so the shape of b ended up matching the shape of a.

There are specific rules that broadcasting follows, which are documented[23] on the TensorFlow website.

The most common use case, and the use case used in all the examples in this course, is broadcasting with scalars. Doing an addition with any scalar value will result in an element wise addition like so:

```
var a = tf.tensor([3, 8, 4, 6], [2, 2]);
var b = tf.scalar(2);
a.add(b).print();
```

This results in:

```
Tensor
    [[5, 10],
     [6, 8 ]]
```

And is equivalent to:

```
var a = tf.tensor([3, 8, 4, 6], [2, 2]);
var b = tf.tensor([2, 2, 2, 2], [2, 2]);
a.add(b).print();
```

Subtraction, Division, and Multiplication

Similar to addition, the sub function performs *element wise* subtraction between two Tensors. The div function performs *element wise* division between two Tensors, and the mul function performs *element wise* multiplication.

 The same shape constraints and broadcasting rules apply to subtraction.

Mean Squared Error

Let's follow on from our Tensor-as-an-Image concept and try to figure out what algorithm we would use to detect if two images are similar to each other?

Let's imagine two Tensors represent black and white images, like so:

```
var a = tf.tensor([200, 176, 3, 34], [2,2]);
var b = tf.tensor([213, 132, 0, 98], [2,2]);
```

 These would be some *very* small images, but the algorithm will work for any size image.

First, we might try subtracting one Tensor from the other. The closer to 0 the resulting Tensor is the closer the images are, like so:

```
a.sub(b).print()
```

This results in:

```
Tensor
    [[-13, 44 ],
     [3  , -64]]
```

The mean of all the values would give us a *single number* that defines how close the images are, like so:

```
a.sub(b).mean().print()
```

This results in:

```
Tensor
    -7.5
```

Comparing the same image with itself returns 0, like so:

```
a.sub(a).mean().print()
```

This results in:

```
Tensor
    0
```

So it might seem at first glance that this algorithm does a good job, but what if we compared b with a instead of a with b, like so:

```
b.sub(a).mean().print()
```

This results in:

```
Tensor
    7.5
```

The result here is positive, whereas the result before was negative. That's not ideal; the order of comparison shouldn't matter. The main issue here is that the Tensor we are averaging has a mixture of positive and negative numbers like so:

```
Tensor
    [[-13, 44 ],
     [3  , -64]]
```

We want all the numbers to be positive, an operation that can help us here is square, if we ran:

```
a.sub(b).square().print()
```

This results in:

```
Tensor
    [[169, 1936],
     [9  , 4096]]
```

And since all the numbers are now positive then the mean won't change regardless of the order of comparison:

```
a.sub(b).square().mean().print()
```

and

```
b.sub(a).square().mean().print()
```

both return:

```
Tensor
    1552.5
```

and comparing a with itself returns 0 like so:

```
a.sub(a).square().mean().print()
```

returns:

```
Tensor
    0
```

In machine learning, you will often have to decide on an algorithm to determine if two *things* are close to each other. For various reasons, *Mean Squared Error* is a good algorithm to use, so it's used frequently throughout this course and in real-life.

Summary

Operations are functions that run on Tensors and return other Tensors. There are many operations.[22] that you can find on the TensorFlow.js website.

In this course, To complete all the example projects, you will only need to know, `add`, `sub`, `div`, `mul`, `mean` and `square`.

[22] TensorFlow.js operations API https://js.tensorflow.org/api/latest/#Operations

[23] Broadcasting rules https://www.tensorflow.org/xla/broadcasting

Optimization

In the chapter "What is a Neural Network?" we covered the concept of training a neural network. This training process is the compute-heavy, number-crunching we associate with machine learning, this training is called **optimization**.

The good news is that this is what TensorFlow.js is good at, in this lecture, we'll cover the mechanics of **optimization** using the low-level core library.

Code

The code for this lecture, and the next lecture on optimization, is in the `tensorflow-optimization` folder in the source code associated with this course.

That folder has three files, like so:

❶ This index.html file loads tensorflow.js and also just the scratch.js file.

❷ This file contains all the completed code for this lecture.

❸ This file should be empty.

Open the index.html as we taught in the setup-instructions lecture and then open the console in the browser, this is where the messages will go.

Add your code to scratch.js and refresh the browser to execute it. If you have problems, check main.js to see the correct completed code.

Use Case

To demonstrate how optimization works, let's take an embarrassingly simple use case, something so simple we can deduce the best value in our minds, and then let's use TensorFlow.js to figure it out for us.

Imagine we have an array [2, -5, 16, -24, 3] we want to multiply each value of the array by a number x so that after the multiplication, they all add up to 0.

If x was 0 then the array would end up looking like [2 x 0, -5 x 0, 16 x 0, -24 x 0, 3 x 0] which results in [0, 0, 0, 0, 0].

If you multiply everything by 0, you get 0. I did mention that this was an embarrassingly simple use case!

We know the optimal value for x is 0, what if x started life as 4.12, how would you use TensorFlow.js to optimize, to *train*, x to become 0?

Variables

We first need to define our values, like so:

```
var x = tf.variable(4.12);
var ys = tf.tensor([2, -5, 16, -24, 3]);
```

x is our variable Tensor, which we create using the special tf.variable function, this tells TensorFlow.js that x is *trainable*.

ys is a Tensor to hold a sample list of numbers.

 Tensors are read-only by default in TensorFlow; once you create them, they cannot change. Variables are different; variables can change over time. We want TensorFlow to optimize x to 0, so we define it as a variable.

Loss Function

In any optimization, there is a *loss* function, a function that returns a number, which indicates how **wrong** we are. In this case, it will return how wrong our value of x is.

In the previous lecture I introduced you to the handy Mean Squared Error equation, we can use that here as our loss function like so:

```
var loss = ys.mul(x).square().mean().print();
```

With a value of 4.12 this initially results in:

```
Tensor
    2953.54541015625
```

With a value of 0 this results in:

```
Tensor
    0
```

With a value of -4.12 this results in:

```
Tensor
    2953.54541015625
```

So we know that if the value of x is trained to below 0, the loss will increase again. The minimum value of our loss will be 0.

Gradient Descent

Another reason to use such a simple use case with one variable is that we can visualize the process in a graph. As you add variables, the number of dimensions of the graph increases, and it becomes harder to reason about.

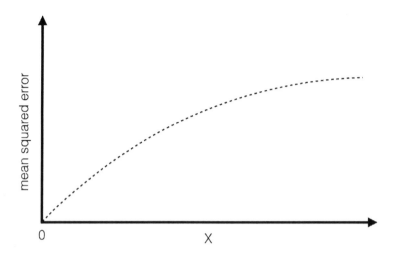

Figure 20. The error curve

On the x-axis, we see values for x. On the y-axis, we see values for the mean squared error. The dotted curve is the loss at different values of 0.

As x moves towards 0, the mean squared error also goes down, our loss goes down, as we go past 0 into negative territory, the number starts going up again.

The lowest point of the curve is the optimal value of x.

We start at 4.12, and we *slide* down the gradient of the curve till we reach the lowest point.

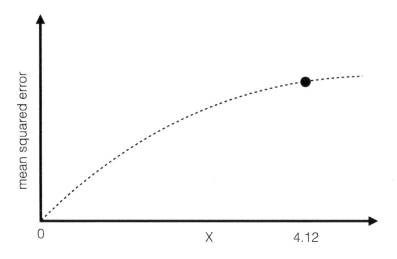

Figure 21. Where is our starting point?

The thing is a computer doesn't know the slope of the curve, so how would it figure out how to slide down it?

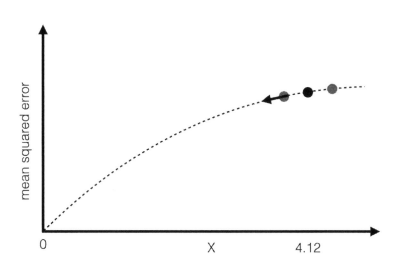

Figure 22. Deciding which way is down towards the least error value

One solution is just to try 4.11 and 4.13 if the loss is less with 4.11, then the curve seems to be sloping down in that direction, so just follow it, perhaps later try 4.10, 4.09.

You keep on doing that until you reach the lowest point, and it starts going up again, then you are reasonably sure you are at the lowest point.

That's called *Gradient Decent*, and it's a conventional algorithm for training Machine Learning models.

Optimizing for one variable is a 2D curve, optimizing for two variables is a 3D surface, the lowest point on that surface is the optimal value of those two variables.

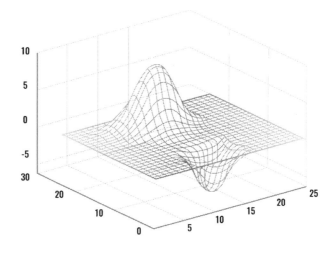

Figure 23. The optimal value for a 3D surface

 Whether you are dealing with one variable or 10,000, there is a surface with a lowest point. The value of all those variables at that lowest point is the optimal set of values.

Optimizer

That's what we are doing theoretically, how do we do it practically with TensorFlow.js? We use something called an `optimizer`.

```
var learningRate = 0.001;
var optimizer = tf.train.sgd(learningRate);
```

We construct an optimizer by using one of the available Training Optimizers[24] in TensorFlow.js. The one above is the Stochastic Gradient Descent[25] (sgd) optimizer, a faster implementation of the Gradient Descent mechanism discussed above.

The sgd optimizer takes as a parameter the *learning rate*; the lower the *learning rate*, the smaller increments it tunes the variables. A large *learning rate* means the training will be fast, but it might never converge to the actual optimum value if it's too large. A small learning rate will train slower but is more likely not to step over the optimum value and converge.

> Choosing the right optimizer requires a much deeper knowledge of Machine Learning than covered in this course. A thorough analysis of these different optimizers and when to use them can be found in the article An overview of gradient descent optimization algorithms[26].
>
>
>
> The TensorFlow.js documentation for all the optimizers, apart from sgd, have links to academic papers discussing the use of that optimizer. For example, adam[27] links to the paper Adam: A Method for Stochastic Optimization[28].
>
> But a simple guide for beginners might be to use sgd for shallow networks without many layers and use adam or rmsprop for bigger networks with more layers.

Once you've created an optimizer, you call optimiser.minimise to perform the optimization. In our use case, we have one variable x which we want TensorFlow.js to try to optimize for us.

optimiser.minimise takes as input a loss function, a loss function that needs to return a *loss* as a Tensor, like so:

```
console.log(x.dataSync());  ❶
optimizer.minimize(() => {  ❷
  return ys
    .mul(x)
    .square()
    .mean();
});
console.log(x.dataSync());  ❸
```

❶ This prints out the current value of x, which at the start should be 4.12

❷ Our `minimize` function which takes as input a loss function, a function that returns a Tensor telling the optimizer how wrong the current value of x is.

❸ This prints out the value of x after optimization.

The loss function **has** to use x somewhere in its calculation, if x isn't used then there is no point optimizing for it, TensorFlow.js will return an error. We used the mean squared error function we have discussed above.

After the single iteration of optimization above the value of x should be different, on my computer with the learning rate of 0.0001, the variable x becomes 3.98, from a starting point of 4.12.

How do we get it to 0? We simply run it again and again with **the same data**. For our example let's run it 200 times with a simple loop like so:

```
var x = tf.variable(tf.scalar(4.12));
var ys = tf.tensor([2, -5, 16, -24, 3]);

var optimizer = tf.train.sgd(0.0001);

console.log(x.dataSync());
for (let i = 0; i < 200; i++) {
    optimizer.minimize(() => {
        return ys
            .mul(x)
            .square()
            .mean();
    });
    console.log(x.dataSync());
}
```

By the end of 200 iterations (*epochs*), I get 0.00345, not zero but close. If I run it 1000 times, I get 1.707e-15.

That's the simplicity of supervised machine learning; you get some data, define a loss function, choose an optimizer, and run it across the data repeatedly until you get the desired outcome. That's training, that's Machine Learning.

Cleaning Up

JavaScript does much of the cleaning up after you. In other languages, if you create a variable, you have to remember to tell the computer when you are finished with it, so it knows it can clean it up and let the memory be used by something else. Tensors, however, use your Graphics Card, your GPU. When using your GPU, JavaScript can't automatically clean up after itself, so you need to clean up after yourself. If you fail to do this, then your application will have a memory leak and will eventually consume all the memory on your computer and die.

There are two methods of doing this, either using the dispose function or the tf.tidy function, let's first look at the dispose function.

```
for (let i = 0; i < 200; i++) {
    var loss = null;
    optimizer.minimize(() => {
        loss = ys
            .mul(x)
            .square()
            .mean();
        return loss;
    });
    loss.dispose() ❶
    console.log(x.dataSync());
}
```

❶ However you do it, make sure after you have finished with a Tensor to call
dispose on it.

This can become tedious and error prone to remember all the Tensors that are
getting created, so TensorFlow.js has a helper function called tf.tidy which you
can use like so:

```
for (let i = 0; i < 200; i++) {
    tf.tidy(() => { ❶
        optimizer.minimize(() => {
            return ys
                .mul(x)
                .square()
                .mean();
            return loss;
        });
        console.log(x.dataSync());
    }); ❶
}
```

❶ We wrap all the code in our app that is creating Tensors with a tf.tidy function
when the inner function returns it automatically deletes all the Tensors that
have been created.

Summary

The process of training a Neural Network is called optimization.

A Neural Network is just a large TensorFlow.js graph of different Tensors and operations performed on those Tensors. Some of those Tensors are read-only; for instance, training data, some of those nodes are `variables`, for example, weights.

An optimizer is the thing that tunes those variables, adjusts them based on the information it gets about how wrong a Neural Network is, information it gets from a loss function.

We can run the optimizer as many times as we want, each iteration we call an *epoch*.

This is how we do supervised machine learning. We run the neural network with some sample data, compare the result it gives with the known good result, calculate a loss, then let the optimizer tune the variables, and then repeat it until we think we have optimized enough.

[24] Training Optimizers https://js.tensorflow.org/api/latest/#Training-Optimizers

[25] Stochastic Gradient Descent https://js.tensorflow.org/api/latest/#train.sgd

[26] An overview of gradient descent optimization algorithms https://ruder.io/optimizing-gradient-descent/

[27] Adam TensorFlow.js Optimizer API https://js.tensorflow.org/api/latest/#train.adam

[28] Adam: A Method for Stochastic Optimization https://arxiv.org/abs/1412.6980

Part IV: Regression

Regression is one of the simplest machine learning algorithms you can build and is a great starting point for understanding Neural Networks. We learn how to use TensorFlow.js to construct a linear and polynomial regression model. We use the lower level Core API to get a good understanding of the internals of TensorFlow.js.

What is Regression?

Regression is a type of analysis that *estimates* the relationship between two or more variables. For example, the sales of a company have a link to the amount spent on advertising. One variable is called a **dependant variable**, and the others are **independent variables**. If both variables are independent, then there is no relationship, it's just two sets of numbers with no influence on each other. In the above example, the sales are *dependant* on the amount of money spent on advertising, the advertising spend is an *independent variable*, and the sales number is a *dependant variable*.

There are different types of relationships; some are linear, which means as the dependant variable changes, the independent variable changes in a straight line.

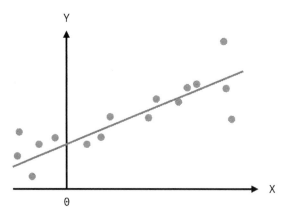

Figure 24. Example Linear Regression

There are also non-linear relationships, which are also called *polynomial*.

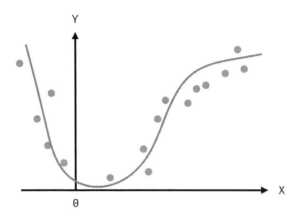

Figure 25. Example Polynomial Regression

If the relationship is more binary, true/false, for instance, then we would use something called logistic regression.

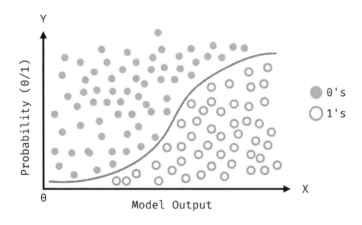

Figure 26. Example Logistic Regression

In this chapter, we are going to cover Linear Regression and Polynomial Regression. Regression is a well-understood problem with some well-known algorithms to solve, so using a Neural Network might seem overkill. However, it's an excellent way to introduce us to Neural Networks since we can model a regression analysis using a *single neuron*.

Linear Regression

Linear regression is the *hello world* of machine learning. It's the simplest predictive modelling you can do, and it's predictive because given an independent value x you can then predict what the dependant value of y will be. For example cricket chirps increase linearly with the independent variable temperature, so if the temperature is 70 degrees fahrenheit, then cricket chirps should be around 120 per minute, at least in Iowa in autumn where this data was collected.

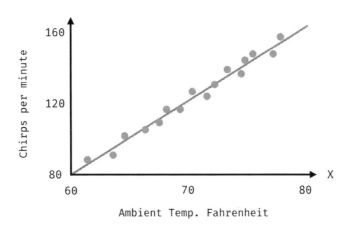

Figure 27. Example linear regression cricket chirps vs. temp.

It's also predictive because you can extend the line *beyond the data* you have, you can extrapolate from the data. So you can use a value for x that you have never seen before and have no data about to predict the value of cricket chirps per hour.

Equation

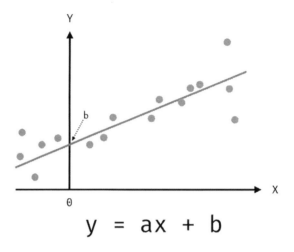

$$y = ax + b$$

Figure 28. Equation of a line

A line is represented by an equation y = a*x + b.

- y is the value you're trying to predict based on the value of x

- b is the intercept of the line to the y axis.

- a defines the slope of the line

x is independent variable, y is the dependant variable, the nature of the relationship is defined by the values a and b. To find the line that best represents a linear relationship between two sets of variables x and y we need to find values for a and b, we call this the *best fit line*.

 It's common in Machine Learning to refer to **x**'s as the inputs to a Neural Network (independent variables) and the **y**'s are the outputs (dependant variables).

One reason for using linear regression as our first proper TensorFlow.js application is that the problem can be represented as a single neuron.

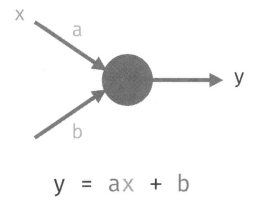

$$y = ax + b$$

Figure 29. Equation of a line represented as an artificial neuron

As long as we have some input data (x) with known good values (y) we can use TensorFlow.js to optimize (train) the values of a and b to find our best fit line.

The application we will be building in this chapter

We could demo this with a set of data such as temperature and cricket chirps, but I find it's easier to understand what's going on when you can play around with the data yourself, adjust, and see how this affects the training and outcome.

So in our demo app you will be making the data points yourself from your own clicks on the screen, you could just as easily load up your own data sourced from somewhere else though.

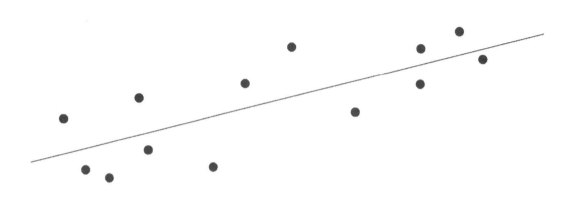

0.01083   312

Figure 30. Completed Linear Regression Application

Every time you click on the screen, you add a data point and it re-trains the values of a and b through 300 executions of optimizer.minimise.

Calculating loss

The first problem we have to deal with in any Neural Network is to figure out how we are going to calculate the loss. The loss needs to be the lowest when our values for a and b are optimal.

Our data is a set of points, of x and y, x is the input and y being the output.

Figure 31. Data set

The best-fit line is made from a series of points with the same values of x as the data points but different values of y, like so:

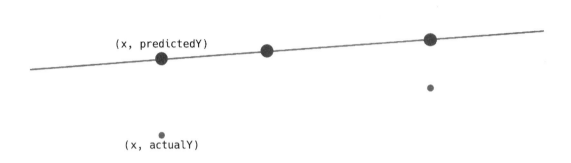

Figure 32. Data set with best fit line

The x values are the same, but the y values are different. I like to call the y values of our data, actualY, and the y values from our model the predictedY. Our model's loss is how far our predictedY values are from our actualY values.

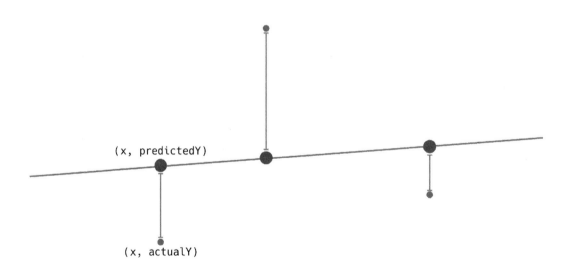

Figure 33. Data set with best fit line and error

In this scenario, to calculate the loss, we can use our trusty Mean Square Error again! We take the actualY from the predictedY, square the result, and then get the average.

Code

Open up the `loss-regression` folder in the demo code folder.

As usual, we have a `start.js` file and a `completed.js` file, we will add our code to the `start.js` file. If you get stuck, check your code against the `completed.js` file.

If you run the `index.html` application now, it will bring up a screen with a line across it; clicking on the screen will add a point; however, nothing else will happen. The application isn't complete.

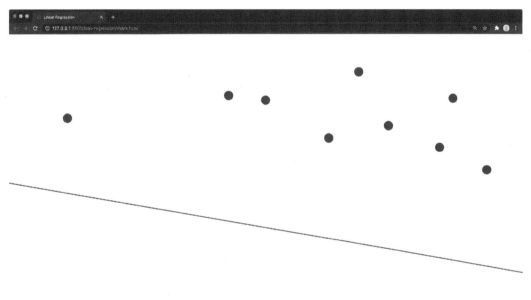

`0.17565`

Figure 34. Loss regression application, can add dots but it doesn't calculate the best fit line

In the code, we've scaled the width and height, so it starts at 0 and finishes at 1. 0 for x means to the far left of the screen, and 1 for x means the far right. Scaling numbers to between 0 and 1 is an excellent habit to get into with Neural Networks; you can always scale them back out to real-world numbers later, but within the confines of a neural network, try to keep the numbers small and contained in the same boundaries as each other.

I've hardcoded values of -0.3 for a and 0.5 for c in our line equation. The negative value for a means it slopes down, and the value of 0.5 for c means it crosses the y-axis half-way up the screen.

In the loss-calculation application, we are going to keep the values of a and c fixed, and our job is to figure out the loss of the application given the points we click on the screen.

Let's take a look at the start.js code first, at the top of the file we have a few variables:

```
let LOSS = 0;      ❶

let Xs = [];       ❷
let Ys = [];

let A = -0.3;      ❸
let C = 0.5;
const calculatePredictedY = x => A * x + C;      ❹
```

❶ This is a helper variable, anything you store in here will be displayed in the bottom left hand side of the screen.

❷ Every-time you click on the screen the mouse x, y points will be appended to these arrays, the Xs in one and the Ys in another.

❸ A and C are the variables that represent our line; if you adjust these, it will change the slope and intercept of the line on the screen.

❹ A helper equation, given the values of A and C if we pass it an x, it will calculate y for us.

Then we have a train function, like so:

```
async function train() {
  calculate_loss()
}
```

Every time you click the mouse on the screen, the application calls the train function; inside that function, we will calculate our loss using TensorFlow.js and store the result in the LOSS variable so that it gets displayed on the screen.

The first thing we need to do is to covert our Xs and Ys data to Tensors, add this to the top of the `train` function:

```
const actualXs = tf.tensor(Xs);
const actualYs = tf.tensor(Ys);
```

 We could use `tf.tensor1d(Xs, [Xs.length, 1])` to be more explicit, however, to keep things simple, I've chosen to leave these out. In your applications, I recommend you keep things explicit.

We will also need to convert the A and C variable to Tensors, like so:

```
const a = tf.scalar(A);
const c = tf.scalar(C);
```

We are using `tf.scalar` here, this is a Tensor for a single value, a single number.

Next up we need to calculate the list of y points for our best fit line, like so:

```
predictedYs = a.mul(actualXs).add(c);
```

This applies the equation of a line all the `actualXs` (y = a*x + c) and stores the results as a 1D Tensor called `predictedYs`.

Now we have a 1D Tensor of `predictedYs` and a 1D Tensor of `actualYs`, we need to calculate the mean squared error between them, like so:

```
let loss = predictedYs
    .sub(actualYs)
    .square()
    .mean();
```

 We've covered mean squared error in-depth in the **Tensors** lecture.

Finally, we need to extract the actual value from the `loss` tensor and store in the normal javascript LOSS variable so it will be displayed on the screen, like so:

```
LOSS = loss.dataSync()[0];
```

Now when you run the application, you'll notice that the number on the bottom left updates as you click around the screen. You know it's working because if you click very close to the line, then the loss will be close to 0. If you click far away from the line, then the loss will be some number >0, give it a try!

The full source for our application looks like so:

```
// Store the loss in this variable and it will be printed on the screen.
let LOSS = 0;

// Every-time you click on the screen the mouse x,y points will be stored
in here.
let Xs = [];
let Ys = [];

// The equation of a line
let A = -0.3;
let C = 0.5;

async function train() {
  const actualXs = tf.tensor(Xs);
  const actualYs = tf.tensor(Ys);

  const a = tf.scalar(A);
  const c = tf.scalar(C);

  predictedYs = a.mul(actualXs).add(c);

  let loss = predictedYs
    .sub(actualYs)
    .square()
    .mean();

  LOSS = loss.dataSync()[0];
}
```

Summary

Before we start to train a neural network, we need to define a loss function, a way of knowing how *wrong* our neural network is.

We calculate the loss as the mean square error of the `actualY` values of the points you click on the screen and their `predictedY` equivalents on the hardcoded best-fit line.

Although we are making our data by clicking on the screen, we would use the same approach when applying linear regression to another data set.

Linear Regression Application

In this lecture, we will build an application that does Linear regression using TensorFlow.js in the browser.

So far we've covered an introduction to regression, an explanation of linear regression and we learned how to calculate loss in a linear regression app. Now we will build the rest of the application, which learns the best-fit-line for our data.

Code

Open up the `linear-regression` folder in the demo code folder.

As usual, we have a `start.js` file and a `completed.js` file, we will add our code to the `start.js` file. If you get stuck, check your code against the `completed.js` file.

 There is also a `ui.js` file, this is the user interface code, which will do the work of drawing lines and text on the screen. We won't be touching the `ui.js` file or explaining its contents. We are using a library called p5.js[29] to create our user interface.

Settings and Variables

Let's first discuss some of the javascript variables at the top of the `start.js` file:

```
// Variables and constants
let LOSS = 0;                ❶
let CURRENT_EPOCH = 0;       ❷
const MAX_EPOCHS = 300;      ❸

// This will store mouse x,y points that have been scaled from 0->1
let Xs = [];                 ❹
let Ys = [];                 ❹

// The equation of a line
let A = Math.random();       ❺
let C = Math.random();       ❺
```

❶ The current loss of the model, whatever we store in here will be displayed in the bottom left hand corner of the screen.

❷ This current epoch, how many times we have run the training on the model. It is displayed in the bottom right-hand corner of the screen.

❸ The max iterations we will try to train the model for each new data point added.

❹ The variables that store the X and Y points.

❺ The variables that represent a line, we initialize them with random numbers.

Training and Loss

Next, let's look at the train function, this gets called every time a mouse is clicked on the screen, and a new data point is added to our collection.

This contains the code from the **Calculating Loss** lecture, that's a good starting point, but we will need to update this to work in our current application.

```
async function train() {
  const actualXs = tf.tensor(Xs);
  const actualYs = tf.tensor(Ys);

  const a = tf.scalar(A);
  const c = tf.scalar(C);

  predictedYs = a.mul(actualXs).add(c);

  let loss = predictedYs
    .sub(actualYs)
    .square()
    .mean();

  LOSS = loss.dataSync()[0];
}
```

First, let's extract the a and c variables and move them to the top of the file. They only need to be created once, but inside the train function, they are created every time the button is clicked, so remove them from the train function.

It should now look like so:

```
async function train() {
  const actualXs = tf.tensor(Xs);
  const actualYs = tf.tensor(Ys);

  predictedYs = a.mul(actualXs).add(c);

  let loss = predictedYs
    .sub(actualYs)
    .square()
    .mean();

  LOSS = loss.dataSync()[0];
}
```

Creating an optimizer

We also need to create an optimizer so let's create that as well. At the top of the file under the other variables add this code:

```
const a = tf.variable(tf.scalar(A));
const c = tf.variable(tf.scalar(C));

const learningRate = 0.5;
const optimizer = tf.train.sgd(learningRate);
```

We are being a lot more explicit now, instead of using `tf.variable(A)` we are using `tf.variable(tf.scalar(A))`. It didn't matter before because we were not using the values of a and c outside, so we didn't care how TensorFlow treated it, but this time we do care, we want TensorFlow to treat it as a single value, so we tell it it's a single scalar value.

We've covered the concept of learning rates and optimizers before; for a refresher, please read the lecture on **Optimization**. In our app, we are using the TensorFlow.js stochastic gradient descent[30] optimizer.

Now we have created the optimizer let's use it to optimise the a and c variables. The optimizer has a minimize function that expects to input a function that returns the current loss of the model. We've got the loss calculation already in our train function so let's just wrap it with `optimizer.minimize(() => { ⋯ });` like so:

```
async function train() {
  const actualXs = tf.tensor(Xs);
  const actualYs = tf.tensor(Ys);

  optimizer.minimize(() => {
    const predictedYs = a.mul(actualXs).add(c);
    let loss = predictedYs
      .sub(actualYs)
      .square()
      .mean();

    LOSS = loss.dataSync()[0];
    return loss;
  });
}
```

This will run one training run across all the data points and calculate new, more optimal values for a and c. If you run this you wouldn't see the line change on the screen, to change the line drawn on the screen we need to update the A and C variables, we can use `dataSync()` function, like so:

```
A = a.dataSync()[0];
C = c.dataSync()[0];
```

The final state of our train function looks like so:

```
async function train() {
  const actualXs = tf.tensor(Xs);
  const actualYs = tf.tensor(Ys);

  optimizer.minimize(() => {
    const predictedYs = a.mul(actualXs).add(c);
    let loss = predictedYs
      .sub(actualYs)
      .square()
      .mean();

    LOSS = loss.dataSync()[0];
    return loss;
  });
  A = a.dataSync()[0];
  C = c.dataSync()[0];
}
```

Training for multiple iterations

If we run our application, as you click on the screen and add data points, you will
see the line change. Every time you click, TensorFlow.js is doing **one single
training iteration** and adjusting the best fit line just from that.

What if we run multiple training runs with **exactly the same data**, can we get
better results? Let's wrap the optimizer code with a loop to see, like so:

```
async function train() {
  const actualXs = tf.tensor(Xs);
  const actualYs = tf.tensor(Ys);

  for (CURRENT_EPOCH = 0; CURRENT_EPOCH < MAX_EPOCHS; CURRENT_EPOCH++) {
    optimizer.minimize(() => {
      const predictedYs = a.mul(actualXs).add(c);
      let loss = predictedYs
        .sub(actualYs)
        .square()
        .mean();

      LOSS = loss.dataSync()[0];
      return loss;
    });
    A = a.dataSync()[0];
    C = c.dataSync()[0];
  }
}
```

await tf.nextFrame

Every time we click, there is a short pause, and things seem to lock up, after about 10 seconds on my computer, I finally see the dot and the best-fit-line appear. The reason for this is that the computer is busy doing all the machine learning training, it's taken complete control, and the browser doesn't have a chance to update the screen until the training has finished.

To give the browser a chance to update the screen, we can use the tf.nextFrame function. This gives a break to the training and lets the browser update before continuing the training again. It returns a Promise that resolves when it's time to continue painting, so we use it together with the JavaScript await function like so:

```
async function train() {
  const actualXs = tf.tensor(Xs);
  const actualYs = tf.tensor(Ys);

  for (CURRENT_EPOCH = 0; CURRENT_EPOCH < MAX_EPOCHS; CURRENT_EPOCH++) {
    optimizer.minimize(() => {
      const predictedYs = a.mul(actualXs).add(c);
      let loss = predictedYs
        .sub(actualYs)
        .square()
        .mean();

      LOSS = loss.dataSync()[0];
      return loss;
    });
    A = a.dataSync()[0];
    C = c.dataSync()[0];
    await tf.nextFrame() ❶
  }
}
```

❶ `await tf.nextFrame` gives the browser a chance to paint the screen.

tf.tidy

We are creating many Tensors in our application. As discussed in the **Optimization** lecture Tensors are not automatically deleted in JavaScript unlike standard JavaScript variables, we need to delete them ourselves, or we get a memory leak.

We could call `dispose()` on all the Tensors at the end of the loop, or we could call `tf.tidy` like so:

```
async function train() {
  const actualXs = tf.tensor(Xs);
  const actualYs = tf.tensor(Ys);

  for (CURRENT_EPOCH = 0; CURRENT_EPOCH < MAX_EPOCHS; CURRENT_EPOCH++) {
    tf.tidy(() => { ❶
      optimizer.minimize(() => {
        const predictedYs = a.mul(actualXs).add(c);
        let loss = predictedYs
          .sub(actualYs)
          .square()
          .mean();

        LOSS = loss.dataSync()[0];
        return loss;
      });
      A = a.dataSync()[0];
      C = c.dataSync()[0];
    })
    await tf.nextFrame();
  }

  actualXs.dispose(); ❷
  actualYs.dispose();
}
```

❶ `tf.tidy` is useful when dealing with lots of tensors that are automatically created due to operations, but can have issues when dealing with async/await and promises so best used wrapped around small sections of code.

❷ We can also use the `dispose` function, it has the added advantage of making the code very clear and easy to understand.

Summary

We put lots of learnings together in this lecture to build our application. We used the loss calculation function we figured out in the **Calculating loss** lecture, we combined it with the learnings from the **Optimization** lecture and built our first machine learning model that does training.

Please take a moment to breathe and congratulate yourself; it took real courage and dedication to get to this point!

You learned what regression is and how to build and train a linear regression model using TensorFlow.js. This demo app uses data you generated from mouse clicks, but you could just as easily use the same model to calculate the best fit line for other fixed data sets.

[29] p5.js https://p5js.org/

[30] stochastic gradient descent https://js.tensorflow.org/api/latest/#train.sgd

Polynomial Regression Application

So far, in this regression chapter, we've covered linear regression. This assumes the relationship between an independent and dependant variable is a straight line, but what if it's not? What if it's a curve? In this lecture I set you the challenge to convert the linear regression application you just created into a polynomial regression application.

The equation for a curve is $y = ax^2 + bx + c$; this is a type of mathematical expression commonly called a polynomial.

$y = ax + b$ is also a polynomial, but it's typically just called a *linear function* because it doesn't have any exponents like x^2, which change it to a non-linear relationship.

The Application

Similar to the linear regression application we built, we will create an app that allows you to create data points and tries to find the best fit curve as above.

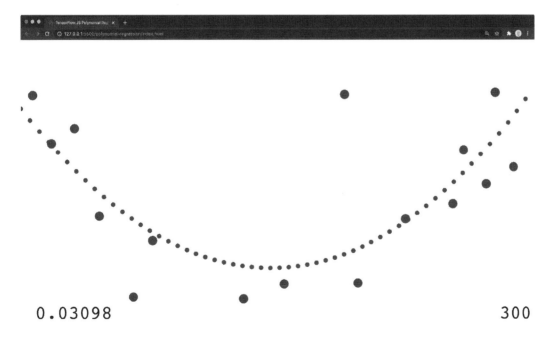

Figure 35. Image of the polynomial example application working

Code

Open the `polynomial-regression` folder in the samples project and run the index.html file as we have done in the previous lessons. The code is very similar in structure to the linear regression application except that `ui.js` has changed to work with curves rather than lines.

Challenge

Open the `start.js` file; we are going to be editing this file to complete the application.

The start.js file looks very similar to the linear-regression application we just built. The challenge I set you now is to convert the linear-regression application into a polynomial-regression application **all by yourself**.

 Scattered through the code are `//TODO` comment blocks, these are strong hints where you should be looking.

So pause at this point, and please give it a go. Doing it yourself will be very rewarding and give you the energy needed to complete the rest of this course.

Solution

The first `TODO` is at the top of the file, we have tensor variables to hold the coefficients for A, and B and we need another to hold C, like so:

```
const a = tf.variable(tf.scalar(A));
const b = tf.variable(tf.scalar(B));
const c = tf.variable(tf.scalar(C)); ❶
```

❶ Add a `tf.variable` to hold c.

The rest of the code is almost the same as the linear regression example apart from two other locations; the first is in the loss function.

Previously the `predictedYs` measured distance from the best-fit-line, we need that line to change to calculate the *ys* as if they came from a curve, like so:

```
const predictedYs = a.mul(actualXs.square())
    .add(b.mul(actualXs))
    .add(c);
```

This applies the equation of a curve $y = ax^2 + bx + c$ across all x values in the tensor actualXs.

The predictedYs are then used in the mean square error loss calculation in the same way as they were in the linear-regression application, so there aren't any code changes there.

Finally since we have another tensor variable c we need to map it's value to the UI variable C to have the curve change on the screen, like so:

```
A = a.dataSync()[0];
B = b.dataSync()[0];
C = c.dataSync()[0]; ❶
```

❶ Extract the value from c and store in C.

Now if you run the application, it should draw the best fit curve instead of a line, try it out!

Summary

With polynomial regression, you can find the non-linear relationship between two variables. The only real difference between the linear regression application and the polynomial regression example is the definition of the loss function. Almost every other part of the application except the UI code is the same.

The loss function is core to machine learning. Picking the proper loss function, and understanding how to define your problem as a loss function is key to building a good machine learning model.

Part V: Neural Networks

In this chapter, we move towards building a deep neural network. We use the MNIST dataset to construct a model that can predict a hand-drawn digit. We cover a few different Neural Network types from a fully connected dense neural network to a much more complex convoluted neural network that is more suited to work with images.

What is MNIST?

In this chapter, we are going to create our first network of neurons or neural network. We'll be creating an application that can recognize handwritten digits, like so:

Figure 36. Example of how the MNIST application will detect that you have drawn the number 2

You draw your digit at the top, and it shows you underneath the number it *thinks* you drew. This is actually a very well known Machine Learning problem called MNIST[31], and it's often used to teach Machine Learning, go ahead and google it you'll find lots of references. It's a great introduction, sophisticated enough so we can do some exciting things but hopefully not too complicated that it's hard to understand, I'll try to break it down step by step as much as possible.

 It's so popular that it's used to measure the relative performance of different Machine Learning algorithms. At http://yann.lecun.com/exdb/mnist/, you will find a list of various Machine Learning algorithms, their success at solving the MNIST problem, and an academic paper where you can learn more about that particular algorithm so you can use it yourself if you want.

We will use two types of Neural Networks to solve MNIST, firstly a straightforward **densely connected neural network**. As we build out this demo app, you will learn how to create a model, train a model, and then use the model, all with the higher level TensorFlow Layers API (so far, we have been using the very low-level Core API). Then we will move onto a more complex model called Convolutional Neural Network (CNN). CNN's are very good at recognizing things in images. The plumbing for the application should remain unchanged, and we switch out the model. That's what is so appealing about TensorFlow; the model can be somewhat abstracted from the training so you can tweak and try out different configurations quickly.

In the next lecture, we will go through how to get the starting code and a brief tour of the initial application. The critical thing to note is that we will focus entirely on the TensorFlow code, the UI code I won't be going through at all.

[31] MNIST http://yann.lecun.com/exdb/mnist/

Setting up the code

Open up the `mnist` folder in the demo code folder.

```
├────── data.js            ❶
├────── helper.js          ❷
├────── index.html         ❸
├────── start.js           ❹
├────── cnn-completed.js   ❺
├────── dense-completed.js ❻
└────── ui.js              ❼
```

As usual, we have a `start.js` file this is where you will add your code. If you get stuck, check your code against either the `cnn-completed.js` file or the `dense-completed.js` depending on where you are in this chapter (it will be obvious).

There are some other files of interest. `data.js` has code that sources and sets up the data to be used in our MNIST application. `helper.js` has various helper functions we will use. There is also a `ui.js` file, this is the user interface code, which will do the work of drawing lines and text on the screen. We won't be touching the `ui.js` file or explaining its contents. We are using a library called p5.js[32] to create our user interface.

Open the index.html as we taught in the setup-instructions lecture and then open the console in the browser, this is where the messages will go.

[32] p5.js https://p5js.org/

Understanding the MNIST training data

At the top of our `start.js` file you will see a function called `loadData`, like so:

```
async function loadData() {
  PROGRESS_UI.setStatus(`Loading...`);
  DATA = new MnistData();
  await DATA.load();
}
```

`MnistData` is the class that contains all the code which we use to gather and prepare the data for our MNIST application. This file is almost an exact mirror of a similar file in the official TensorFlow.js MNIST demo application. All the code for `MnistData` is in the `data.js` file. We won't go through in-depth the contents of that file, but there are few critical points of knowledge it would be helpful to understand in more depth.

Features & Labels

The type of machine learning we are covering in this book is Supervised Machine Learning. This means we give our machine learning model a collection of training data (features) and what we expect the model to output for each set of that training data we pass in (labels). From just those two pieces of information, it learns how to give the correct answers (labels) for a given set of inputs (features).

Imagine studying for school with just the exam papers and solutions, no actual lessons. We do the same here; we are giving it the exam papers (features) and the exam solutions (labels), and the model then learns how to answer exam questions (assign the right label for a set of features). In the future, we can give it an exam paper (set of features) it has never seen before it will provide you with hopefully a pretty good answer (label).

Given that, the data we need to train our machine learning model is a set of images of hand-drawn digits (the features) as well as the actual digit drawn in the image (the label).

I'm being meticulous in using the words **features** and **labels**. That is the language used in all machine learning models and writing, get used to thinking in terms of the **features** of some data and the **label** you want to associate with those features.

Features, the hand-drawn digits

At the top of data.js we see two interesting variables:

```
const MNIST_IMAGES_SPRITE_PATH =
  "https://storage.googleapis.com/learnjs-data/model-
builder/mnist_images.png";
const MNIST_LABELS_PATH =
  "https://storage.googleapis.com/learnjs-data/model-
builder/mnist_labels_uint8";
```

MNIST_IMAGES_SPRITE_PATH is a PNG that contains all the images hand-drawn digits. You can open it up in your browser; it might take a second to load but should end up looking something like so:

Figure 37. What the MNIST feature data set looks like zoomed out

It's a very long thin image, if you zoom into the image, you will see something like so:

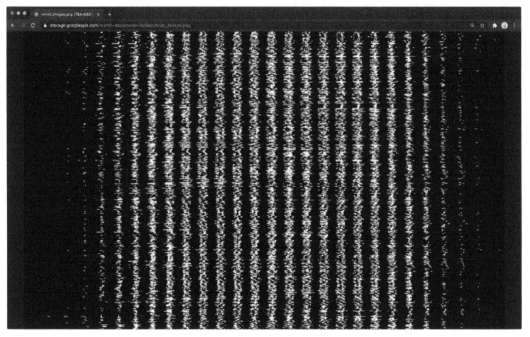

Figure 38. What the MNIST feature data set looks like zoomed in

It still doesn't look like an image of a hand-drawn digit. The data is a single 28 by 28 pixel image of a digit spread like butter into one layer of 784 pixels. Each *row* in that image is, therefore, a single digit, and the entire image contains 65,000 digits. So the png file is a 784 x 65,000 pixel image.

This file gets loaded by the load() function, eventually after some processing all the data gets stored in a variable called datasetImages like so:

```
this.datasetImages = new Float32Array(datasetBytesBuffer);
```

The critical thing to realize is that even though the source is a 2D image, the datasetImages variable is that it's a *single dimensional array* with all the image data. One big long array of 784 x 65,000 = 50,960,000 numbers, which, when added up, equals about 50mb of memory.

If we then look further down that file to getTrainData() we can then see how we use that Tensor shape parameters to load up the data as a 1D source and provide the shape, like so:

```
const xs = tf.tensor4d(this.trainImages, [ ❶
  this.trainImages.length / IMAGE_SIZE, ❷
  IMAGE_H, ❸
  IMAGE_W, ❸
  1 ❹
]);
```

❶ The source of all the image data, as a 1D array

❷ The number of images

❸ The height and width of the images (IMAGE_H and IMAGE_W are 28)

❹ These are black and white images, so only one is needed for each *pixel*. If these were color images, we might have three here for each of Red, Green, and Blue.

 It's far easier in TensorFlow to store your data as a 1D source and then use the shapes parameter when creating tensors to add dimensionality.

Labels, the numerical digit of each image

What number is each image though? That's what the file in MNIST_LABELS_PATH contains. I wouldn't open it up, however since it's a binary file and will show junk on the page!

It contains 65,000 entries, one for each image, but the format might seem a little strange at first, it uses something called *one hot encoding*.

Instead of using the numerical value of 9 to represent an image of 9. It represents the number as an array of 10 numbers, but the numbers can only be 0 or 1, like so:

0,0,0,0,0,0,0,0,0,1
0 1 2 3 4 5 6 7 8 9

Figure 39. 9 represented as a one-hot encoding format

This isn't *binary*, only one of the elements can be 1 all the others have to be 0, the number it represents is based on where the 1 is in the array, like so:

The number 9 is represented as [0,0,0,0,0,0,0,0,0,1] The number 8 is represented as [0,0,0,0,0,0,0,0,1,0] The number 7 is represented as [0,0,0,0,0,0,0,1,0,0]

We have this approach because we are going to use a loss function called `categoricalCrossEntropy`.

 A full dissection of categorical cross-entropy is beyond the scope of this introductory book. However, I can give a high-level overview, just like a car, you can achieve a lot only by understanding how to use it rather than the details of how it works.

In our first demo application in chapter two, we discussed *Classification Outputs* when using the MobileNet model. With classification type problems, models output a set of probabilities, and it's up to you to decide if the probability is good enough to take that answer.

For the MNIST application, it's the same; it's going to output a set of probabilities for each of the ten possible labels, like so:

```
.32, .02, .05, .02, .04, .08, .12, .03, .02, .78
 0    1    2    3    4    5    6    7    8    9
```

Figure 40. The output of the MNIST model as a probability distribution

This results in an output that looks like a probability distribution; we see that the model predicted a 78% probability that the number in the image is 9.

categoricalCrossEntropy is a good algorithm for calculating loss functions for probability distributions. If given two two probability distributions, it calculates how far off they are from each other.

When we use [0,0,0,0,0,0,0,0,0,1] to represent the numerical digit 9 we are saying that there is a 100% probability that it's a 9 and 0% probability it's any other number, one-hot encoding in this use case is a probability distribution.

So when you are building a classifier model, something that can classify things in buckets, the output is usually going to be a probability distribution, so the labels for the training data will need to be another probability distribution called one-hot encoding.

Taking a look at the code in the load() function, we can see our labels are created as another 1D array, like so:

```
this.datasetLabels = new Uint8Array(await labelsResponse.arrayBuffer());
```

This array will be 65,000 rows, each containing a one-hot encoding representation of a digit so that it will be size 65,000 * 10.

Later on in our `getTrainData()` function we can see the labels are loaded into a Tensor like so:

```
const labels = tf.tensor2d(this.trainLabels, [ ❶
  this.trainLabels.length / NUM_CLASSES, ❷
  NUM_CLASSES ❸
]);
```

❶ The source data for our labels,

❷ The first param of our shape is the number of records, this calculates down to 65,000

❸ The second param of our shape is the number of "things" our model can predict, the size of our probability distribution, and the corresponding one-hot encoded labels, NUM_CLASSES is 10 in this case.

Test/Train Split

One thing to note in the file is that we have two functions to get formatted data, one called `getTrainData()` and one called `getTestData()`.

When it comes to supervised machine learning, it's good to keep some of your data back to validate that the model will work well in the real world and is not *over fit*. We call the data we will train our model with **training data** and the data we are going to validate our model with, **test data**.

So we train with the training data then once we think training is complete, we run it through some test data to validate, we don't train the model with this test data, we are just double checking that if we give it some data it's never seen before, it will still function well. If the accuracy during training gets to 95% and when running on fresh test data it drops to say 60%, we can conclude that the model has been overfitted. It understands the training data so intimately that it's learned to make good guesses. However, when given some data it has never seen before, it fails.

We've configured at the top of the file a variable `NUM_TRAIN_ELEMENTS`, which is equal to `55000`.

In our example, we reserved 10,000 of the 65,000 total examples for testing, and we are going to be training with the other 55,000.

Summary

We spent a long time discussing the source data for our example application, and we've now starting to see Tensors used in more real-world scenarios. Keeping the source data as a 1D array and applying shapes via Tensors to give the data more meaning.

We also talked about how these simple classification models output probability distributions. To train, we need to use the `categoricalCrossEntropy` algorithm, which in turn requires the labels for the training data set to be probability distributions, which is why you'll see one-hot encoding used in input data sets, like ours.

Finally, we spoke about the test/train data split, how we reserve some data to be used only for validating our model might work in the real work and has not been over-fit.

We will use several different model algorithms and architectures in our example application, but all the training data will remain the same.

This is going to be your journey into Machine Learning, get a good source of data, make it clean, and structure it thoroughly. Then, you can try out several different Machine Learning architectures and settings until you get something that works for you.

Creating a densely connected Neural Network

We're ready to build our Neural Network, which will learn to recognize hand-drawn digits. We are going to start with a simple model, that also happens to work surprisingly well, called a densely connected neural network.

To explain this, let's work with a simplified example, like so:

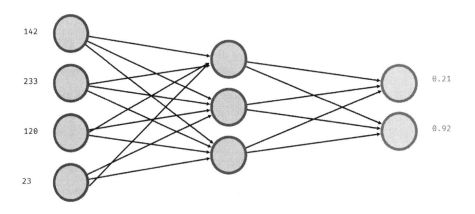

Figure 41. An example of a three-layer densely connected neural network

We have three layers, one input layer of 4 nodes, one output layer of 2 nodes, and one hidden layer of 3 nodes. Each of the black lines are *weights*, which we train and use to transform the inputs to the outputs.

The reason it's **densely** connected is that a weight connects each node to each node in the next layer, so each node has an input from every single node in the previous layer.

We could write this using the TensorFlow Core API the same way we used in the previous demo application, it's possible but would require much boilerplate code.

Instead we are going to start using the TensorFlow Layers API, this abstracts us from the lower level implementation details and allows us to more easily build neural networks which are composed of layers of neurons. In fact to represent the simple neural network above only requires 4 lines of code, like so:

```
const model = tf.sequential(); ❶
model.add(tf.layers.flatten({ inputShape: [4, 1] })); ❷
model.add(tf.layers.dense({ units: 3,activation: "relu" })); ❸
model.add(tf.layers.dense({ units: 2,activation: "softmax" })); ❹
```

❶ We use the TensorFlow helper function to create a sequential model.

❷ We add the first layer, which takes as input four values (4 *rows* of one value each), flatten forces the inputs into a 1D array.

❸ We add our hidden layer of 3 nodes. We also define an activation function of relu. This is just a scaling function that determines what number the node emits as an output. We discussed these in the starting **What is a Neural Network?** lecture. dense means we also create weights between each node in the previous layer and node in this layer.

❹ We add our output layer of 3 nodes, this time we use another activation function called softmax, we will discuss this in more detail later.

As you can see, creating Neural Networks with the TensorFlow Layers API is much easier than with the Core API, however it's essential to understand that what's going on underneath is the same as with the Core API. The framework is still creating nodes with weights represented as Tensors and Tensor Variables, and later on, we will still be using a loss function with an optimizer. The key point here is that a lot is now abstracted away for you into a line of code.

Completing our code

The example above was for a simple four input and two output Neural Network. For our MNIST example application, we need to have 784 input nodes, one for each pixel value of a 28 x 28 x 1 image of a digit and we need a 10 node output layer, one for each potential value the image could be out of the set "0,1,2,3,4,5,6,7,8,9".

The code changes are minimal however, inside the createDenseModel() function in the start.js file just write this code:

```
const model = tf.sequential();
model.add(tf.layers.flatten({
    inputShape: [IMAGE_H, IMAGE_W, 1] ❶
}));
model.add(tf.layers.dense({ ❷
    units: 42,
    activation: "relu"
}));
model.add(tf.layers.dense({ ❸
    units: 10,
    activation: "softmax"
}));
return model; ❹
```

❶ IMAGE_H and IMAGE_W are both 28, from our previous lecture you'll recognize this as the *shape* of our input data, we need to take this and flatten it to a 1D input layer of 784 nodes.

❷ We create a 42 node dense hidden layer, why 42? Why not! Pick another see if it works better :)

❸ The final output layer needs to be 10 nodes. softmax is an activation function which turns a set of numbers into a probability distribution, since we are building a classifier and using the categoricalCrossentropy loss function we need the output to be a probability distribution. Details like this are in the TensorFlow API docs[33] for each loss function.

❹ Remember to return the model you've created.

Summary

You've now created your first Neural Network. It doesn't work yet; we still have some more code to write but well done for getting here!

We learned what a densely connected Neural Network is, and we created one using the TensorFlow Layers API. In the next lecture, we will cover how to train this model using the training data we've already prepared.

[33] TensorFlow API docs https://js.tensorflow.org/api/0.12.0/#losses.softmaxCrossEntropy

Training a Neural Network using the Layers API

In the previous lecture, we covered how to create a straightforward model for our neural network, in this lecture we are going to pull that together with our training data to train it and do some machine learning.

Code

We've covered training *concepts* in previous lectures, so in this lecture, we will show how to implement those concepts with code and again using the TensorFlow Layers API.

We'll be fleshing out the `trainModel()` function in `start.js`

The first thing we need to add to the top of the function is to get a reference to the model we created in the last lecture, like so:

```
MODEL = createDenseModel();
```

We are storing this in a global variable called `MODEL` since we need to use that in other functions in the file.

 Global variables are not a great example of how to architect an application. I am using them to keep the supporting code simple so we can focus on machine learning.

Compiling the model

Before we start training a model, we need to *compile* it. compile[34] does several things, but mostly this is where we let TensorFlow know the type of optimizer we are going to use and the loss function.

Next up in our file add this code:

```
MODEL.compile({
  optimizer: "rmsprop", ❶
  loss: "categoricalCrossentropy", ❷
  metrics: ["accuracy"] ❸
});
```

❶ Previously we've used the sgd optimizer, for our MNIST example we are going
to use the rmsprop optimizer since it performs better with problems like these,
for more details about how this optimizer works reads the paper linked to the
rmsprop docs[35]. You can pass in a string such as "rmsprop" or pass in an
instance like new tf.train.rmsprop(···) You can fine-tune the optimizer by
passing it values in its constructor; for our example, we are happy to use the
defaults.

❷ The loss function we are going to use is called categoricalCrossentropy. For the
layers API, there is a list of Training Losses[36] you can use,
"categoricalCrossentropy" is the string version of softMaxCrossEtropy[37].

❸ The layers API gives us a way to interrogate the training and useful metrics
after each run, and we provide a list of the types of metrics we are interested in
here.

Training the model

Before we train the model, we need the data, to get a reference to the training data
from our MnistData object, add this line of code:

```
const trainData = DATA.getTrainData();
```

trainData is an object with two properties, xs are the features, the images we are
going to train with, and 'labels' are the one hot encoded versions of the digits in
each corresponding image.

Next up, in between the "Training Start" and "Training Complete" log lines add
this code:

```
await MODEL.fit(trainData.xs, trainData.labels, { ❶
  batchSize: BATCH_SIZE, ❷
  validationSplit: VALIDATION_SPLIT, ❸
  epochs: EPOCHS ❹
});
```

❶ The fit function is the primary function that performs the training of our model, we pass it the training data.

❷ The amount of data in our training set, 55000, is substantial. If we tried to train in one attempt, we would run out of memory on our computer. Instead, we break up the data into smaller batches and run through one batch at a time. BATCH_SIZE in our application is set to 320, so it will train with 320 example images at a time.

❸ When breaking up your training into multiple smaller batches, it's good practice to keep some data behind as a validation that the batching process itself hasn't caused issues with the training. It's the same reason we keep back some of the data for testing once the model has completed training. VALIDATION_SPLIT is set to 0.15, which means 15% of the 320 examples are used to validate that the batching isn't causing problems.

❹ epochs is the number of times we want to loop through all training data, the number of iterations. EPOCHS is currently set in the file as 1, but feel free to experiment and set it to a higher amount.

Testing the model

After we have completed the training, we want to perform a final test of the model with data it has never seen before. This gives us an indication of how the model will work in the real world with real data.

We add this code to the end of the trainModel() function:

```
const testData = DATA.getTestData(); ❶
const testResult = MODEL.evaluate(testData.xs, testData.labels); ❷
const testAccPercent = testResult[1].dataSync()[0] * 100; ❸
console.log(`Final test accuracy: ${testAccPercent.toFixed(1)}%`); ❹
```

❶ We get the test data from our MnistData class, same as the training data, this contains xs and labels.

❷ The evaluate function runs those inputs through the model and the loss function but importantly doesn't perform any training. We want to figure out how accurate the model is.

❸ This is some simple formatting to get data from testResult and turn it into an accuracy percentage.

❹ We print this out to the console.

Running the application

If we open up the application, make sure to open up the console, press the train button, and see some information printed out like so:

```
Training Model
 Training Start
 Training Complete
Final test accuracy: 90.1%
```

We now have a trained model with a test accuracy of 90.1%, pretty accurate for one epoch, and a very naive densely connected neural network.

Interrogating the training

The UI for our application didn't change at all. We pressed *LOAD*, and the only way to know what was happening in training was to wait for it to end and see what is logged to the console. We want to see what's happening during training and perhaps update the UI accordingly, and TensorFlow.js has something that we can use called callbacks.

If we go back to our fit function and just after epochs properly let's add another called callbacks with code like so:

```
await MODEL.fit(trainData.xs, trainData.labels, {
    batchSize: BATCH_SIZE,
    validationSplit: VALIDATION_SPLIT,
    epochs: EPOCHS,
    callbacks: {
      onBatchEnd: async (batch, logs) => { ❶
        trainBatchCount++;
        let percentComplete = (
          (trainBatchCount / totalNumBatches) *
          100
        ).toFixed(1);
        PROGRESS_UI.setProgress(percentComplete);
        PROGRESS_UI.setStatus(`ACC ${logs.acc.toFixed(3)}`); ❷
        console.log(`Training... (${percentComplete}% complete)`);
        await tf.nextFrame(); ❸
      },
      onEpochEnd: async (epoch, logs) => { ❹
        valAcc = logs.val_acc;
        console.log(`Accuracy: ${valAcc}`);
        PROGRESS_UI.setStatus(`*ACC ${logs.val_acc.toFixed(3)}`);
        await tf.nextFrame();
      }
    }
});
```

❶ The onBatchEnd callback gets called at the end of each smaller 320 sized batch of training. It gets passed some useful parameters like logs, which contains numbers like the current training accuracy of the model and others.

❷ We turn the accuracy into a percentage and use some helper UI code, so it's shown on the screen on the top right of our application.

❸ We use await tf.nextFrame() so the browser has a chance to pause and draw the progress on the page before continuing with the training.

❹ onEpochEnd is very similar, it gets called at the end of an entire epoch. Once all the data has been looped through once.

When you press the LOAD button in the application, you should see a progress bar appear to the right of the button at the top of the page and visually see the application's progress as it goes through the training process.

Summary

We learned how to perform training using the layers API, how to use the `compile` function to prepare our model with the optimizer and loss function we are going to use, and how to use the `fit` function to perform the training. We later learned how to use `callbacks` to interrogate the model during the training process.

Next up, we are going to learn how to use the model in a real-world setting. We are going to draw a number and have the model try to predict what number we drew.

[34] compile https://js.tensorflow.org/api/latest/#tf.LayersModel.compile:

[35] rmsprop docs https://js.tensorflow.org/api/latest/#train.rmsprop

[36] Training Losses https://js.tensorflow.org/api/latest/#Training-Losses

[37] softMaxCrossEtropy https://js.tensorflow.org/api/latest/#losses.softmaxCrossEntropy

Using a TensorFlow model in inference mode

In the previous lectures we learned how to create and then train a neural network using TensorFlow, in this lecture we will learn how to use that model in *inference mode*. *Inference* refers to the process of using a trained model to make a prediction.

Code

If we look in our `start.js` file we'll see a function called `inferModel` like so:

```
function inferModel(data) {
  console.log({
    data
  });

  // TODO
}
```

The function needs to be fleshed out, it gets called by our application when we press the green "Check" button in the application. The application first scales your digit to 28 by 28 pixels and then converts it into a 1D array then called the `inferModel` function and passes in as `data` a 1D array of the image.

We want to pass this `data` to our TensorFlow model and extract it's prediction, that's the goal of this function.

First convert `data` into a Tensor like so:

```
let inputs = tf.tensor4d(data, [1, 28, 28, 1]);
inputs.print();
```

 The dimensionality of the inputs to the model need to match the dimensionality of the training data.

When we trained the model we passed in training data with this shape `tf.tensor4d(data, [55000,28,28,1])` since we were passing in a Tensor that contained 55,000 images. Even though we are now passing in just one image we still need to pass in a 4D tensor so the first parameter is 1 lie so ` [1, 28, 28, 1]`.

Next we take this inputs, pump them into the start of our model and capture the outputs it pumps back out like so:

```
const output = MODEL.predict(inputs);
```

output is a Tensor and if you remember is not a single number, we are expecting an array of 10 values each which contains a probability of the image being one of those categories. To extract those values we need to call dataSync like so:

```
const distribution = output.dataSync();
console.log({
    distribution
});
```

distribution now contains a standard JavaScript array which we can print out, like so:

```
distribution: Float32Array(10)
0: 0.015741486102342606
1: 0.0006235429318621755
2: 0.8232827186584473
3: 0.13048334419727325
4: 0.0009772877674549818
5: 0.0022565999533981085
6: 0.00227708974853158
7: 0.001965487375855446
8: 0.021101541817188263
9: 0.00012907495256513357
```

The first thing to notice about the distribution is that all the numbers add up to 1, that's because it's a probability distribution, with this type of model no matter how many categories you use the end probability distribution has to and should add up to 1.

The second thing to notice is the the value for the 2nd index is the highest, it's 0.82. That's because the image I drew was of a number 2 so the model predicted correctly.

So there is a little semantic interpretation that needs to happen, the model outputs some numbers and you need to convert that to a real world meaning, since we trained the model with the 2nd index being 2 thats the meaning of this set of outputs.

The final few bits we need to do are just to display this information in the user interface, let's actually get the predicted number from our array of probabiliities like so:

```
const prediction = getPrediction(output)
console.log({
  prediction
});
```

getPrediction is a helper function, you can find it in the helper.js file, it just loops through the array and finds the index with the highest value and returns that prediction.

Before we leave this function let's remember to clean up our Tensors, we need to do this so we don't have a memory leak:

```
inputs.dispose();
output.dispose();
```

Finally this function needs to return an object with both the prediction and distribution, like so:

```
return {
  prediction,
  distribution
};
```

Summary

Using a model is much easier than training one in the first place, it's called using a model in *inference mode* and involves pumping in data the same dimension of the training data and extracting the outputs. There may have to be some manipulation of the outputs to extract human meaning from the numbers but that depends on the nature of your machine learning model.

Convolutional Neural Networks

So far, we've learned how to implement MNIST using a straightforward, densely connected neural network. It's simple to understand and implement; however, the predictive capacity has limits as can be seen from the previous example, it does not always, or even often, predict the correct number. There are many other types of neural networks you can create to solve this problem. One common type of neural network for solving image classification problems, which MNIST is an example of, is a Convolutional Neural Network (CNN).

A CNN model contains several layers of varying styles. Some are called convolution layers, and some are pooling layers, and then some are what we've seen so far as densely connected layers. Then we have the output predictions layer, which is the same as the densely connected neural network we created previously.

We'll explain what each of the different layer types is and what function they serve. I think a CNN model goes a long way to explaining the power of neural networks and why they are so good at solving several seemingly incredibly hard problems.

Visualizing a CNN

A great application that helps you visualize how a CNN works is An Interactive Node-Link Visualization of Convolutional Neural Networks[38]. I recommend you spend a little time now navigating that site. Draw a number and then hover over the individual pixels in the different layers in the 3D representation to the side to see how the data is aggregated up to the top layer, which is the ten output tensor we learned out in the previous lectures.

Convolution

The first type of layer in a CNN is a convolutional layer, which contains several *convoluted features*.

A *convoluted feature* is a matrix which we multiply across the original image (again that is just a matrix) to generate a new matrix. This is an excellent visualization of a feature:

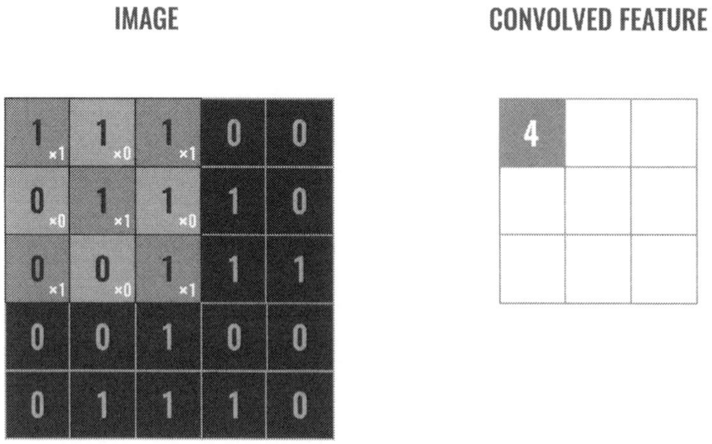

IMAGE

CONVOLVED FEATURE

Figure 42. Start

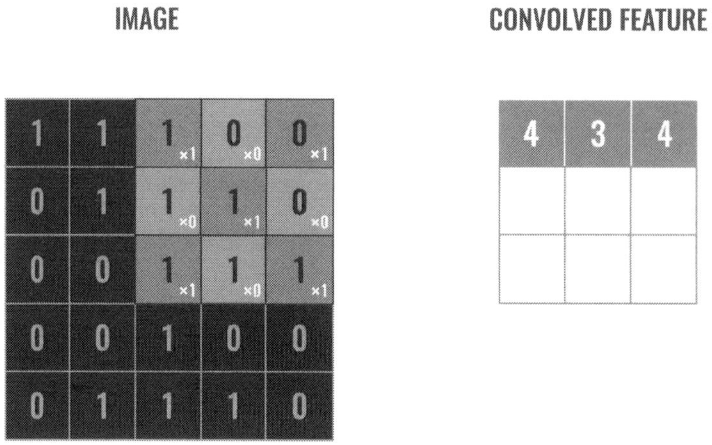

IMAGE

CONVOLVED FEATURE

Figure 43. Somewhere in the middle

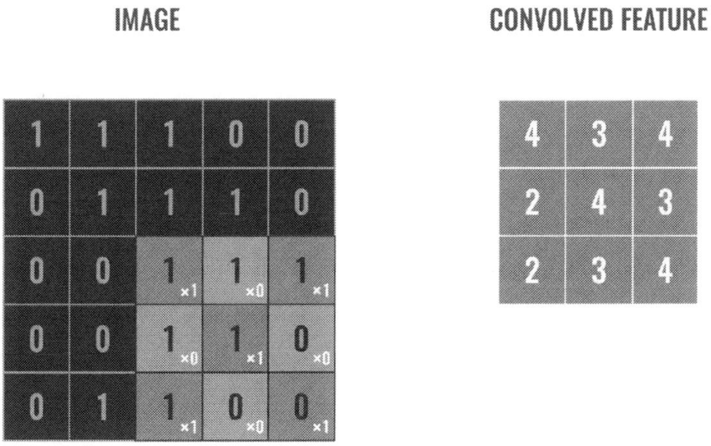

Figure 44. Finish

I'm willing to bet you've used a feature like this many times, probably today. It's how we manipulate images in photo apps, for instance, if we wanted to sharpen an image we may use a feature like so:

$$\begin{bmatrix} 0 & -1 & 0 \\ -1 & 5 & 1 \\ 0 & -1 & 0 \end{bmatrix}$$

Multiplying an image with the above matrix results in a new sharper image, like so:

Figure 45. Sharpening an image

So each convoluted feature results in a new image with some data highlighted. The above feature sharpens an image. Other features may find edges or curves or a vast myriad of different things.

So the first convolution layer in a CNN has a set of such features, each feature creates a new image with some data highlighted.

Some features might be more useful than others to solve certain types of problems. For example, to solve our MNIST problem, we may need features that highlight straight lines and others that highlight curves to highlight and distinguish different features of digits.

What features should you pick?

Given the type of problem you are trying to solve with this neural network, what are the features you want to pick? This is where things get very interesting; you don't choose the features, the neural network evolves the features during a training process; it learns to highlight certain parts of the images.

Each feature is just a set of weights, like so:

$$\begin{bmatrix} w1 & w2 & w3 \\ w4 & w5 & w6 \\ w7 & w8 & w9 \end{bmatrix}$$

Like other weights in a neural network, it is initialized to a set of random numbers, like perhaps so:

$$\begin{bmatrix} 0.21 & 0.01 & 0.56 \\ 0.47 & 0.15 & 0.76 \\ 0.96 & 0.02 & 0.41 \end{bmatrix}$$

Over time, as we train the model, it tweaks the weights in the feature, learning to highlight parts of the image and hiding others.

How we represent this in TensorFlow is with a layer declaration like so:

```
tf.layers.conv2d({
    inputShape: [28, 28, 1], ❶
    kernelSize: 3, ❷
    filters: 16, ❸
    activation: "relu" ❹
})
```

❶ This is the shape of the image, the input data we want to run the convolution over.

❷ This is the size of the filter, so 3 means a 3x3 matrix.

❸ This is the number of filters we want to create so that this layer will output 16 copies of the input image with a different filter applied to each.

❹ Also, we add an activation function, in this case, relu, to each layer - it will scale the output values according to the relu function.

The above layer definition hides much complexity for us; it's creating underneath 16x3x3 = 144 different weights! Each of these weights will need to be tuned by our neural network model.

Pooling

The above results in an explosion of images, with 16 features each input image results in 16 copies, this also means you need 16 times the memory on your computer to hold all that data. That's one of the challenges of CNNs, they require a lot more memory and proportionally a lot more training since there is an increased number of weights that need to be tuned.

One solution to this is pooling, and the concept is quite simple, we resize an image to a smaller image, like so:

Figure 46. Pooling applied to an image makes a smaller image

We scan over the input matrix and *summarize* the information into a single number that we store in the output matrix, like so:

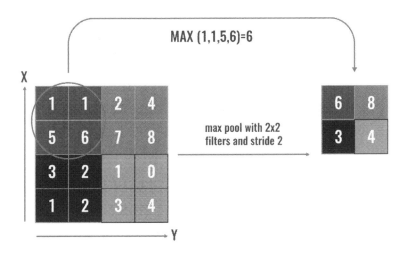

MAX (1,1,5,6)=6

max pool with 2x2
filters and stride 2

Figure 47. Pooling represented as a matrix operation

Does a smaller image still have enough information so we can extract meaning, it's not a question of size or resolution, it's a question of information? How can we summarize the information, so it takes up less memory but is still useful for downstream parts of the Neural Network.

The **stride** determines how many boxes to skip per iteration through the source matrix. There are several functions we can apply to the source numbers, **max** is a good one, whatever the max number in the input matrix use that for the output matrix, but you can use others, like average for instance.

The TensorFlow.js API has a list[39] of pooling layers you can create. To create a max pooling layers like the one described above we use layer declaration like so:

```
tf.layers.maxPooling2D({ ❶
    poolSize: 2, ❷
    strides: 2 ❸
})
```

❶ This is a pooling layer that uses the max function to summarize the information.

❷ The input window; in this case, it will be a 2x2 matrix.

❸ How the input window will iterate across the input matrix will move two cells across each iteration.

The above will result in an output image, which is half the width and height, essentially reducing the image size and memory requirements by 1/4.

A more detailed and thorough explanation of pooling can be found in this article What is max pooling in convolutional neural networks?[40]

Summary

A human brain determines what's inside a picture by looking for features. We have a complex set of filters in our mind which processes images as they come in, throws away most of the information, and gives us summaries to our mind, which decides what we are looking at. CNN's are doing the same thing; the convoluted features extract information from the input sources to highlight the bits we need to understand. This is one reason why CNNs are used in ML so much for image processing and sound processing; they mirror the ways our brains work.

It's a sophisticated methodology to understand, we've barely scraped the surface, but I think you can see the power of TensorFlow.js is that with a few lines of code you can create a very powerful model.

[38] An Interactive Node-Link Visualization of Convolutional Neural Networks https://www.cs.ryerson.ca/~aharley/vis/conv/

[39] list https://js.tensorflow.org/api/latest/#Layers-Pooling

[40] What is max pooling in convolutional neural networks? https://www.quora.com/What-is-max-pooling-in-convolutional-neural-networks

Solving MNIST with Convolutional Neural Networks

Now we have the basis of understanding CNNs let's pull it together to create a CNN version of our MNIST problem.

We will flesh out the function `createConvModel` in `start.js` to create our CNN. That should be all that's needed; the rest of our demo application remains the same. We first need to remember to create a convolutional model instead of our dense model, so replace:

```
MODEL = createDenseModel();
```

with

```
MODEL = createConvModel();
```

in our `trainModel` function.

We've covered the CNN concepts in the previous lecture, so we will now explain how to leverage those concepts in our demo application.

Next inside our `createConvModel` function paste this code:

```
const model = tf.sequential();
model.add(
    tf.layers.conv2d({ ❶
        inputShape: [28, 28, 1],
        kernelSize: 3,
        filters: 16,
        activation: "relu"
    })
);
model.add(
    tf.layers.maxPooling2d({ ❷
        poolSize: 2,
        strides: 2
    })
```

```
    );
model.add(
    tf.layers.conv2d({ ❸
        kernelSize: 3,
        filters: 32,
        activation: "relu"
    })
);
model.add(
    tf.layers.maxPooling2d({ ❹
        poolSize: 2,
        strides: 2
})));

model.add(
    tf.layers.conv2d({ ❺
        kernelSize: 3,
        filters: 32,
        activation: "relu"
    })
);

model.add(
    tf.layers.flatten({}) ❻
);

model.add(
    tf.layers.dense({ ❼
        units: 64,
        activation: "relu"
    })
);

model.add(
    tf.layers.dense({ ❽
        units: 10,
        activation: "softmax"
    })
);

return model;
```

❶ The first layer of the convolutional neural network plays a dual role; it is both
the input layer of the neural network and a layer that performs the first

convolution operation on the input. It receives the 28x28 pixels black and white images. This input layer uses 16 filters with a kernel size of 5 pixels each. It uses a simple RELU activation function.

❷ We use our first `maxPooling2d` layer to downsample the data.

❸ We now add another convolution layer, this time with 32 filters.

❹ We again use max-pooling to downsample the data.

❺ And we add another convolutional layer with another 32 filters.

❻ Now we flatten everything, this turns the complex multi-dimensional input shape into a 1D output shape of 1000's of weights.

❼ We need to summarize this information so we can get to just 10 numbers, so we first create a densely connected layer that turns the 1000's of inputs into 64 outputs.

❽ Our last layer is a dense layer with 10 output units, one for each output class (i.e. 0, 1, 2, 3, 4, 5, 6, 7, 8, 9). Here the classes represent numbers, but it's the same idea if you had classes that represented other entities like dogs and cats (two output classes: 0, 1). We use the softmax function as the activation for the output layer as it creates a probability distribution over our 10 classes, so their output values sum to 1.

Running the above application, we should hopefully result in a **slightly** more accurate version of the application.

Improving MNIST

We've covered a few different methods of solving MNIST in this chapter. It's a great solid introduction to Machine Learning, but it's also just the beginning. You may have noticed that although the accuracy from the test data is relatively high, 90%+, the real-world accuracy from recognizing **your** hand-drawn digits is much lower.

In this lecture, I'll discuss some methods you may want to employ to improve your model's performance.

 They are just pointers; there is no code in our sample repository for you to look at. I'll leave it as an exercise for you to explore and examine, in real life this is how you will work to improve the models you create, enjoy!

Input Normalization

The model was trained on a set of very normalized images; the shape and orientation of the handwritten digits are always the same. It's written with a pen, whereas you will probably be trying to write with a mouse or track-pad, so your hand-drawn digits don't quite look the same as the images in the data set.

One way you can try to improve the result is to make sure the input image is as close to the trained data as possible.

1. Center the digit

Figure 48. Centering a digit

2. Crop it to a square bounding box and then scaling up

Figure 49. Cropping a digit to a bounding box and then scaling

3. Rotate the drawing, so the digit is always vertical

Figure 50. Rotating the digit so it is vertical

Data Augmentation

The solution above talks about how to change the input data to make it look as close as possible to the training data. On the flip side, we can turn the training data to make it more representative of the various ways people can write digits. This is called **data augmentation**.

Take your source data set, and for each image, create slightly different versions.

1. You can try scaling the digits smaller and larger.

2. You can try shifting them a few pixels left and right.

3. You can try rotating them slightly clockwise and anticlockwise.

4. You can try corrupting the images somewhat, delete pixels, add a pixel in other places.

5. You can try to change the color or gray-scale values.

There are lots of ways you can adjust an image. Try to make the adjustments something that will be likely to happen in real life with the application rather than random, e.g. flipping by 90 degrees is perhaps unlikely with the application we are building here.

Create a new data set, much larger than the first with the images adjusted somehow, and run the model with the new data-set.

There are some helpful tools out there that can help create these adjusted images, imgaug[41] is one of them, but if you search for Data Augmentation Tools Machine Learning or something along those lines, you will find others.

Different Algorithms

There are many many different algorithms and collections of layers and methods you can use to solve MNIST.

Kaggle.com is an online platform where people compete to solve ML problems, like MNIST, to score the highest accuracy. There is a fantastic discussion[42] on Kaggle about the different algorithms you can use and the maximum accuracy that can be achieved for MNIST. I recommend you have a read of that it might give you some ideas for other things you can try.

 Kaggle works on a system of honesty, there are ways to fake the results of your ML algorithm, and there are lots of fake results on the platform. If you look at the MNIST leader-board[43] on Kaggle, you'll see a whole page of people who claim to have scored 100% accuracy, which is impossible. If you look at their code, all they are doing is passing through the test data as model outputs without any machine learning.

[41] imgaug https://github.com/aleju/imgaug

[42] fantastic discussion https://www.kaggle.com/c/digit-recognizer/discussion/61480

[43] MNIST leader-board https://www.kaggle.com/c/digit-recognizer/leaderboard

Part VI: Transfer Learning

In this final chapter, we pull all we have learned together and build a model using a decapitated pre-trained model that we employ in conjunction with another model trained from scratch. Transfer learning requires a lot less training data and a lot less computation, so it is ideal for JavaScript and browser-based work.

What is Transfer Learning?

Think of the type of Machine Learning we have been doing so far as teaching a person JavaScript from scratch. Transfer Learning like teaching JavaScript to a Python developer.

It's the transfer of knowledge from two related domains. As humans, we do this all the time. For example, if you can ride a motorbike, you have at least some of the knowledge needed to learn how to drive a car. If you are very good at playing the piano, you will probably find it easier to learn how to play the guitar than someone who has never played any instrument.

An excellent explanation for why this is so powerful is when we dig into how a CNN works.

With Convolutional Neural Networks (CNN) we create convoluted features that are trained to highlight certain features in images. We can work backward and give a model an image and have it tell us what each of those convoluted features highlights in that image.

If you were to example the internal layers of a CNN that has learned how to classify faces. You might see how each layer has learned how to highlight different parts of the input image; the hidden layers learn to recognize more sophisticated features.

For a thorough reading on the internal workings of a CNN, I recommend reading the paper Visualizing and Understanding Convolutional Networks[44].

If we wanted to create an app that recognizes specific hand signals, we could start with a labeled data set of pictures of people making hand signals and the associated meaning (label) and then train the model from scratch. What if instead of starting from scratch, we start with a model that already knows how to recognize other things in images and then retrain it to recognize hand signals?

The MobileNet model we used in the first application we built is an ideal model to retrain. It can recognize 1000 things in the world; the hidden layers have learned to highlight things like lines, curves, and other features. It's only the last layer that pulls this information together and makes a classification into one of the 1000 things.

In transfer learning, we essentially *decapitate* the source model, which means we strip off the last few layers, and then attach onto it a new fresh model. During training, we may choose to retrain the source model, or more commonly, we leave those weights as is and train the new model we attached to it.

We start with a pre-trained model, like so:

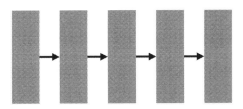

Pre-Trained Model

Figure 51. A 5 layer pre-trained model

We decapitate it, which means we strip off the last layer and that the outputs from a previous layer as the inputs to a new, untrained model, like so:

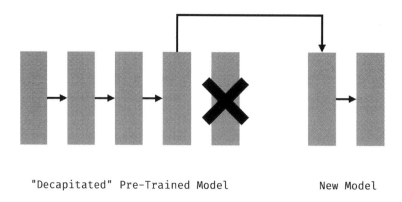

"Decapitated" Pre-Trained Model   New Model

Figure 52. Attaching a 2 layer untrained model to a decapitated pre-trained model.

Through this approach, we have a few advantages:

1. Retraining can be much faster and require a lot less computational power. You're going to see in the application we build that the app is useful with very little training needed.

2. You don't need a massive amount of training data. In the application we are going to build with just 50 or a few 100 sample images, we get some fantastic results.

In this chapter, we will build a hand-sign recognizer application that uses transfer learning with a base decapitated MobileNet model with a new type of classifier attached to it called a KNN model. More on that in the next lecture.

[44] Visualizing and Understanding Convolutional Networks https://arxiv.org/pdf/1311.2901.pdf

What is a KNN classifier

Throughout this course, I've been focussing on Neural Networks, but there are a whole host of other Machine Learning algorithms you can use. Neural Networks are an excellent general-purpose tool, but there are many others. To go beyond this introductory material, you will need to dedicate a fair amount of time to build your tool chest, just like any master craftsman. One other tool I will explain here is what's called a KNN classifier, or a K-nearest neighbor classifier.

They are relatively easy to understand however their predictive power on their own is limited, in combination with a neural network, though as part of a transfer learning model, they can be handy and effortless to use.

How does it work?

Given a set of labeled data points, we can predict the label of a new data point by just looking at the other examples that are the closest to it.

For example, imagine we have this clustering of dots, some are labeled as solid, and some are labeled as hollow. If there was a new dot at the star's position, what is the likely label of that new dot?

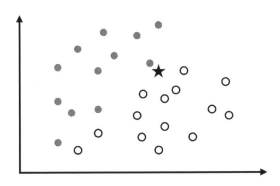

Figure 53. Which label is the black star, solid or hollow?

We could figure out the distance between the new dot and all the other dots and then copy the label of the closest dot, but in this case, it looks like it might get mislabelled because although it's close to a solid dot, it feels like it's part of the hollow dot cluster.

Maybe a better solution is to figure out the most common label from say the closest 5 dots, or the closest 10 dots.

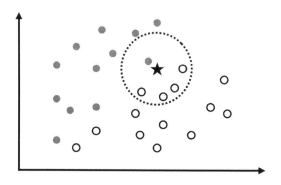

Figure 54. Pick the most common label from the closest 5 dots

The K-factor

The number of other examples to compare with that is the K number in KNN classification.

There is usually an optimum value for K for each data set; you can figure it out by looking at a labeled data set, splitting it into a training and validation data set. Then use increasing values of K and see how well they predict the validation data set.

You may end up with a result like this, which indicates that a value of 7 is suitable for this data set.

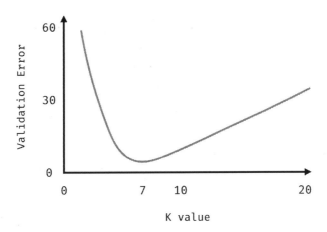

Figure 55. Example of the validation error with different values of K

Choose the K value with the lowest error.

Calculating distance between data points

In our example above, we use a simple 2D graph with data points. It's easy for the mind to *see* the distance between two data points in the 2D world. What about 3D, or 5D or 1000D? It gets harder to visualize, but the algorithm is just the same: Euclidian distance[45].

Another way to look at the data in our dot examples above is a data set with two features: an x value and a y value.

Suppose we wanted to use KNN for other types of problems the data points would need to be able to be mapped onto points in a Euclidean space. That means the features of the points need to be numbers.

One example of a problem you can use KNN with is the Iris Flowers dataset[46]. This data set involves predicting the specific flower species of the genus Iris from different measurements of Iris flowers.

The data set has 150 data points, where each data point has:

1. Sepal length in cm.

2. Sepal width in cm.

3. Petal length in cm.

4. Petal width in cm.

5. Class

So each data point has 4 features and 1 class. Each of the features is a number (cm), so it can be mapped into Euclidean space, and you can calculate the distance between and data point and any other in this Euclidean space.

Summary

This was a quick lecture to cover the concept of the KNN classifier. They are simple machine learning models that are simple to understand, simple to implement; however, their predictive power is limited. However, used in conjunction with a neural network in a transfer learning model, they can become much more powerful. We will be using a KNN classifier as the new machine learning model to add on top of a decapitated neural network in the next lecture.

[45] Euclidian distance https://en.wikipedia.org/wiki/Euclidean_distance

[46] Iris Flowers dataset http://archive.ics.uci.edu/ml/datasets/Iris

Transfer Learning with MobileNet and KNN

In this lecture, we will use Transfer learning to retrain the MobileNet model to recognize hand signs (or any other images) instead.

The surprising thing for everyone **I hope** is just how easy this is going to be; the whole app is less than 100 lines of JavaScript. If I had asked you just to write those 30 lines then you would have had a practical application but not understood anything about how it works.

Now you'll be able to recognize all the power in your fingertips with the APIs and Libraries you are using, and you'll also be able to tweak this example or build others just as powerful all by yourself.

 For this application, you will need a web camera.

Emoji Trainer

The application we are going to build is called "Emoji Trainer". You can teach it to associate images with certain emoji. E.g., you can train it to show a thumbs up emoji when you put your thumb up to the camera, like so:

Figure 56. Using the Emoji Trainer with thumbs up

Or you can train it to recognize a one-handed heart symbol like so:

Figure 57. Using the Emoji Trainer with heart

Code

Open the emoji-trainer folder in the sources project, and let's take a quick look at what you will find.

```
├──── README.md
├──── assets/
├──── completed.js
├──── index.html
└──── start.js
```

assets contains some CSS files needed to style to application. completed.js is the final code; you can compare what you create with this file to see if you missed anything. start.js is the starting file; we will be fleshing this in this lecture. index.html this is where we load the dependant javascript files and packages.

index.html

If you open index.html you'll find we import a number of dependencies, like so:

```
<script src="https://cdn.jsdelivr.net/npm/@tensorflow/tfjs"></script>
<script src="https://cdn.jsdelivr.net/npm/@tensorflow-
models/mobilenet"></script>
<script src="https://cdn.jsdelivr.net/npm/@tensorflow-models/knn-
classifier"></script>
```

First, we load the TensorFlow JS library, and then we load the MobileNet model since we'll be using that also as a base, and finally, we load the KNN classifier package, which we will use to retrain the final layer.

The rest of the HTML file are UI controls for the application itself.

start.js

If you open start.js, you will find some boilerplate code, and we will be fleshing out all the sections marked // TODO.

At the top of our file you will see some global variables, like so:

```
// Global Variables
let KNN = null;
let MBNET = null;
let CAMERA = null;

// Config
const TOPK = 10;
```

KNN and MBNET reference where we will store the models. CAMERA is a reference to the webcam we will be using in the app. TOPK is the K factor we discussed in the previous lecture, we've set it to 10, but you may want to tweak this to a number that works for you.

main

At the bottom of the file, you will see a main function, and we will begin there.

At the top of the main function we need to load both our MobileNet and KNN classifier so we can use them in our application like so:

```
// Setup Models
console.log("Models Loading...")
KNN = knnClassifier.create(); ❶
MBNET = await mobilenet.load(); ❷
console.log("Models Loaded")
```

❶ We create an instance of the knnClassifier and store it in our KNN variable. knnClassifier isn't a *model*. It's more of a utility package that handles the creation of a knnClassifier for you, i.e., there is no data for the knnClassifier to load up over the network, which is why there is no await keyword used here.

❷ We load up the MobileNet model, we use await since this makes a call over the internet for the dependant data, we will wait for that to load before continuing with the application.

Next, in our main function, we want to initialize our camera. We can do this using standard HTML browser APIs, but it's a little long-winded so the TensorFlow team created a simple one liner in the TensorFlow.js library that handles all of this for us, like so:

```
// Setup WebCam
let videoElement = document.getElementById("webcam");
CAMERA = await tf.data.webcam(videoElement);  ❶
```

❶ This is the line we need to add, this sets up the camera and makes it available to us via the CAMERA variable.

Training

To train our model, we make sure the camera is looking at the hand sign we want to associate with an emoji, and then we press the RECORD button next to the emoji, like so:

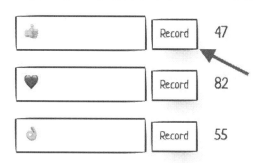

Figure 58. Pressing record grabs snapshots every 100ms to use as training data

Every 100ms the RECORD button is pressed; it takes a snapshot of the camera and uses it to train the model, the total number of snapshots are printed to the right of the RECORD button.

 Do some experimentation with the number of snapshots required to give good predictions. You'll be surprised at how good a model you can create with a minimal training data set. This is one of the critical advantages of Transfer Learning.

The code which grabs the snapshot and trains our model can be found in the setupButton function in start.js, so let's flesh that out.

The setupButton function comes already with a fair amount of code attached, like so:

```
function setupButton(id) {
    let timerId = null;
    let btn = document.getElementById(id + "-btn")
    let span = document.getElementById(id + "-text")
    let input = document.getElementById(id + "-input")

    btn.addEventListener("mousedown", () => {
        let text = input.value;
        let count = 0;
        timerId = setInterval(() => {
            // TODO

            console.log(count)
            span.innerText = count;
            count++;
        }, 100)
    })
    btn.addEventListener("mouseup", () => {
        // Stop grabbing samples of images
        clearTimeout(timerId);
    });
}
```

This code is a lot of boilerplate, which grabs specific values from the HTML like the text inside the input field next to the button; this is what the text variable contains.

 This emoji you are training the model to recognize are just values of an input field. I've defaulted them with my emoji; you can change to whatever emoji you want, or even only text.

It then listens for mouse down on the record button and starts an interval timer, which calls some code every 100ms. We will be fleshing out the // TODO in this function, but it also does some other useful things like incrementing the number displayed to the right of the record button.

The mouseup listener cancels the timer, so the inner training function doesn't get called anymore.

Now le's flesh out the // TODO, replace it with this code:

```
// Start grabbing an image of the video
const image = await CAMERA.capture(); ❶
// Pump it through mobilenet and get the logits
const logits = MBNET.infer(image, true); ❷
// Add this as a bit of data for knn
KNN.addExample(logits, text); ❸
```

❶ We grab a snapshot from the webcam.

❷ We first need to pump it through a decapitated MobileNet model, more on that in the next section. `infer` in this case returns an array of 1024 numbers which we store in `logits` (We'll explain logits soon).

❸ This adds a single data point to our KNN classifier, logits, in this case, is a 1024 array set of numbers. This is a 1024 dimensional space, and those 1024 numbers define a point in that 1024 dimensional space. `text` is the label to associate with that point.

In those three lines of code, we have implemented transfer learning!

Before we leave this function let's not forget to dispose of our Tensors so we don't have a memory leak. After the last line in the snippet above add this:

```
// Delete memory
image.dispose();
if (logits != null) {
    logits.dispose();
}
```

Decapitated Model

The critical line in the above piece of code is is `MBNET.infer(image, true)` so let's spend a moment to unpack it.

`MBNET` takes as input an image and outputs an array of 1000 numbers, which indicate what the image might contain.

Each index in that array is associated with a "class", a thing the image might be. The numbers in the array are related to the probability of that class being what's in the image. If the number is high for that index, the model thinks that class is what is in the image.

If you used `MBNET.infer(image)` all by itself, it would return the values for that last layer, the 1000 length array of probabilities.

Passing `true` as the second parameter returns the output numbers for the layer just before the last layer.

This is usually called the `logits` layer, the last neuron layer of neural network for classification task which produces raw prediction values as real numbers ranging from [-infinity, +infinity], see more on Wikipedia about Logit[47].

In our case, this is a layer that outputs 1024 numbers, ranging from -infinity to +infinity.

Even though 1024 is much higher than the 2 or 4 point examples we used in the KNN lecture, the logic is still the same. Instead of 2D space, we now have a 1024D space. Each set of 1024 numbers is a point in this 1024D space, and you can find the distance between any two points in this space using the euclidean distance algorithm, so KNN works!

We are stripping out the last layer in the MobileNet model (decapitating the model) and taking the outputs of the new output layer and using that as inputs into a new model. It could be another neural network model, but we are using a KNN model.

We are not retraining the MobileNet model, it is read-only for us. We are just getting the logit layer outputs and using them as inputs to a KNN classifier, which we are training.

Using the new combined MobileNet/KNN model

So now we've trained our new model, let's use it. In our application, we click the *RUN* button when we are ready for the application to start making predictions based on the camera input. When the RUN button is pressed in the application, the `run` function is called in `start.js` which should currently look something like so:

```
async function run() {

    let output = document.getElementById("output-result")

    setInterval(async function predict() {
        // TODO
    }, 100)
}
```

Every 100ms it calls the function predict above, which we will flesh out to do some prediction. Paste the below code into the body of the predict function:

```
const numClasses = KNN.getNumClasses(); ❶
if (numClasses > 0) {
    const image = await CAMERA.capture(); ❷
    let logits = MBNET.infer(image, true); ❸
    const res = await KNN.predictClass(logits, TOPK); ❹
    console.log(res)
    output.innerText = res.label; ❺
    // Delete memory ❻
    image.dispose();
    if (logits != null) {
        logits.dispose();
    }
}
```

❶ getNumClasses returns the number of labels the KNN classifier has been given, this should return 3 for our application, it will return 0 if we have not started the training process.

❷ We grab a snapshot from the camera.

❸ We get the outputs from the decapitated MobileNet model.

❹ predictClass predicts the class of this new image given the examples we have already trained the KNN classifier with, i.e., it tells us which emoji it thinks the image is associated with.

❺ This prints the new label (the emoji) to the screen on the application.

❻ We remember to free up the memory.

Summary

We've covered a lot in this lecture, and the most crucial part was understanding what a decapitated model it and how to use it in transfer learning.

Try it out, and you'll see some incredibly powerful application features with a relatively small amount of code.

Machine Learning typically takes considerable computation, so at first glance, browser-based or even JavaScript-based machine learning seems questionable. With this transfer learning example, I hope you've found a use case where machine learning in the browser appears feasible and very possible. Let your minds go wild and explore, take any other machine learning model, and use transfer learning to retrain it to do something related. It's possible to build some incredibly useful applications with something like that.

[47] Logit https://en.wikipedia.org/wiki/Logit

Part VII: Summary

Congratulations on completing *Introduction to Machine Learning with TensorFlow.js*. In this final lecture, we'll quickly review the different lectures, and I will leave you with some final thoughts and where to go next to continue your learning.

Review

Part 1 - Introduction

We talked about the future of JavaScript and Machine Learning and why you might want to learn about the union of these two technologies. I introduced you to the concept of Neural Networks themselves with a simple example and introduced you to TensorFlow and TensorFlow.js. We also covered the setup instructions for all the code samples in this book.

Part 2 - Using a pre-trained model

We built our first application using the pre-trained MobileNet model. We then drilled into the MobileNet model in-depth and discussed how it might take inputs and the actual output of the MobileNet model.

Part 3 - Tensors

Before we can begin to build and train our models, we need to dig into the raw building blocks of TensorFlow, Tensors. We covered how to create them, the operations you can perform on them, and a standard method of calculating the error between two arrays, Mean Squared Error. We then covered TensorFlow.js itself and demonstrated how to use TensorFlow to learn the optimum values for variables in a function.

Part 4 - Regression

Regression is one of the simplest machine learning algorithms you can build and is a great starting point for understanding Neural Networks. We learned how to use TensorFlow.js to construct a linear and polynomial regression model. We used the lower level Core API to get a good understanding of the internals of TensorFlow.js.

Part 5 - Neural Networks

In this chapter, we move towards building a deep neural network. We used the MNIST dataset to construct a model that can predict a hand-drawn digit. We covered a few different Neural Network types from a fully connected dense neural network to a much more complex convoluted neural network that is more suited to work with images.

Part 6 - Transfer Learning

In this final chapter, we pull it together and build a model using a decapitated pre-trained model that we employ in conjunction with another model trained from scratch. Transfer learning requires a lot less training data and a lot less computation, so it is ideal for JavaScript and browser-based work.

Continuing Learning

The purpose of this book is to teach you a practical introduction to Machine Learning. To have at least *some* skills that you can apply today in your work. If you would like to learn more about Machine Learning, I would recommend a few approached depending on what your overall goal is.

If you want to stick to JavaScript, then a good next book is Deep Learning with JavaScript[48]. It's written by several people who have worked on the TensorFlow.js product inside Google. It gives you an excellent more in-depth dive into the framework and covers more foundational algorithms.

If you want to keep it practical like this book, then my recommendation is to dissect the other example applications in the TensorFLow.js examples repository[49] . That's how I learned TensorFlow.js; it's my favorite method of learning. The example apps are well commented, but there is little in the way of documentation.

I recommend just going ahead and building something, anything, using TensorFlow.js - start using it for something that is the best way to learn how to use it practically.

If this book gave you the bug to turn this into a career for you, then I recommend transitioning over to Python. Most of the other courses and training materials in Machine Learning are in Python, and you'll find a lot more support. The concepts are the same, so don't worry, you won't be starting from scratch.

Two fantastic courses that I recommend taking a look at if you want to pursue this further are:

- **Machine Learning** (https://www.coursera.org/learn/machine-learning) This is a famous Machine Learning course by Andrew Ng. He is the co-founder of Coursera and professor at Stanford University. The course is a deep dive into Machine Learning, so be prepared to put much effort into it, but this will give you an excellent bedrock to jump-start your career.

- **Practical Deep Learning for Coders** (https://course.fast.ai/) If you would prefer to keep it practical, then this course on fast.ai is a tremendous next step also.

[48] Deep Learning with JavaScript https://www.amazon.co.uk/Deep-Learning-JavaScript-Shanqing-Cai/dp/1617296171/

[49] examples repository https://github.com/tensorflow/tfjs-examples

Final Words

I want to thank everyone who supported me, my Kickstarter backers, my wife, and my family. Finishing off this book has been a challenge during COVID-19 but, at times, also a welcome distraction. If you want to stay in contact, please follow me on Linked-in (https://www.linkedin.com/in/jawache/) or Twitter (https://twitter.com/jawache).

Cheers,

Asim

Printed in Great Britain
by Amazon